KNOW YOUR AURA—
KNOW YOUR SELF!

Your aura is a fascinating and useful key to your personality—a remarkable tool for self-exploration and growth. Now, you can determine the color of your aura with the "Personality Spectrums" Questionnaire. There are no right or wrong answers, just a choice of five responses— from "This does not describe me" to "This is me!"—to 98 unique personality statements, such as:

- You feel compelled to do something significant with your life.
- You are not "free and easy" when spending your money on others.
- You express your sexuality in a creative, inventive, and experimental manner.
- You are a nonconformist.
- When making a decision, you try to find a solution that pleases everyone.
- You are slow to choose friends.
- You meet physical challenges without fear.

Discover *your* personality color today, with . . .

WHAT COLOR IS YOUR AURA?

BARBARA BOWERS is the director and founder of Barbara Bowers Consultants, Barbara Bowers Design and Life Color, Inc., and has served as a personnel management consultant for FORTUNE 500 companies and as a consultant and team builder for various school districts. A former high school teacher and guidance counselor, she has served as educational consultant for the California Council for Social Studies, the University of California system, and the University of Idaho at Boise.

For more information concerning business consulting services or speaking dates, address inquiries to: P.O. Box 2434, Del Mar, California 92014

What Color Is Your Aura?

Personality Spectrums for Understanding and Growth

Barbara Bowers, Ph.D.

POCKET BOOKS

New York   London   Toronto   Sydney   Tokyo

To G., G., and A. T. I.

I thank you for my life.

An *Original* publication of POCKET BOOKS

 POCKET BOOKS, a division of Simon & Schuster Inc.
1230 Avenue of the Americas, New York, NY 10020

ISBN: 0-671-66084-5

First Pocket Books trade paperback printing January 1989

10 9 8 7 6 5 4 3 2 1

POCKET and colophon are trademarks of
Simon & Schuster Inc.

Manufactured in Spain.

Acknowledgments

This book represents an overwhelming outpouring of love and support from a great many people who worked on it with me. I am deeply grateful. Thank you.

I especially want to thank Allan Roshon, who saw the same vision I saw and then went to work helping to build the questionnaire and record all the test results. He has been my mentor, my teacher, and my friend.

Jim Shores and Garret Annofsky loaned me their computers and trained me to use the word processing software so that I could get this book written.

I want to express my deep love and appreciation to Doretta Winkelman for managing the office while I took time to write this book. And thanks also to Sinthia St. Martin, who served as Doretta's assistant. They truly empowered me to take my risk.

I owe a deep debt of gratitude to my close network of friends, clients, and area coordinators who have consistently encouraged and emotionally supported me. You are numerous. You know who you are and I thank you from the bottom of my heart.

Contents

ONE

THE HUMAN RAINBOW

This is a book about the human aura and the personality attributes revealed by the rainbow of colored light that surrounds the body. The aura is the electromagnetic energy field that emanates from all living things. The colors and patterns within this energy field constitute a kind of blueprint of a person's soul, a chart of the individual's potential. From my experience seeing the aura, I have developed a system that I call Personality Spectrums to assist people in finding their pathway to a full and productive life. I have written this book to share with you the information I see in the aura, and to help you see how it will allow you to take charge of your life.

For the past five years I have been a consultant using the Personality Spectrums system to work with individuals, families, school districts, businesses, and nonprofit organizations. The purpose of my work is to help people know themselves better, communicate more effectively, and find direction for their lives. People who know the color of their personality are able to make decisions, implement changes, and take risks— not out of fear or anger, but from the power that comes from knowing themselves. I work to help people act on ideas and internal impulses that they know to be congruent with the truth about themselves.

For many years I was a high school social science teacher and career counselor. I observed the endless struggle of students striving to achieve their own identity, not knowing how to go about getting what they truly wanted out of life. Too often I saw them trying to live according to their parents' dreams and ideals instead of acting on their own inner sense of themselves. As a career and vocational guidance counselor, I often asked them to consider their choices from the perspective of what would make them happy, what would give them a sense of fulfillment and well-being. It was obvious to me which students were acting in harmony with the energy I saw around them (the aura) and which students were acting in opposition to that energy.

I have always seen the human aura. Ever since I can remember, I have been able to see the luminescent colors around people. Because I was not familiar with the phenomenon known as the aura, I assumed that everyone saw what I saw. I was well into adulthood before I realized my error. At first I thought this ability to see what, as a child, I called the "pretty lights" led to my intense fascination with color and my interest in art—the use of color, the interaction between color and light, and the psychology of color. In pursuit of my artistic interests, I took classes on color theory. As a result of this study, I discovered that I have the gift of "color memory," the ability to remember color over both time and distance. (Most people are able to remember color for three seconds or three feet, which is why one carries a skirt or a pair of slacks around a department store in order to match accessories.) I was also given the Color-Matching Aptitude Test* which determined that I can see and differentiate fifty thousand hues, tints, and values of colors. Most people who have not been trained in color can see only a very narrow range of about five thousand colors.

Although I have been able to see the aura and have used what it told me about people all my life, both as a teacher and an artist, the development of the Personality Spectrums system took many years. In the end, the key to, or meaning of, each of the colors in the aura spectrum came to me, all at once in a kind of epiphany. In that single moment of revelation—an "aha" moment—I realized how the correlative elements of the aura organize the colors into an integrated psychological pat-

---

*Inter-Society Color Council, Color-Matching Aptitude Test (Philadelphia: Federation of Societies for Coatings Technology, 1978).

tern. At first I was unaware of the vastness and complexity of the pattern; but over time and with the help of professional therapists who worked along with me to refine Personality Spectrums, I began to comprehend the structure of the system that I saw as radiating bands of colored energy.

At the same time I began to peruse the available literature on auras. But nothing seemed to help me understand what I saw and what I knew. I was looking for something that would do more than describe the physical reality I was seeing. I wanted to be able to understand the system that seemed to be the basis for what I saw.

Many of the books gave me only a vague sense of what the authors thought an aura was. Some called it a halo. Others referred to it as the ectoplasm. Still others thought it was the afterimage they saw after they stared at an object too long. Some of the writers delved into the esoteric and psychic aspects of the aura. A few authors focused on the aura as a diagnostic tool in determining physical health patterns. Others discussed the colors in the aura from the perspective of the seven chakra centers, or the seven rays. No book focused on the deep psychological patterns of behavior, character, and personality that I saw represented by the bands of color within the aura.

Most of the literature about the auras seemed to have as its basis Eastern philosophy, spirituality, and mysticism. The writings were helpful because they confirmed that the aura was real, that other people saw the aura, and that the colors and patterns within the aura contained coded information.

When I could not find anyone who could discuss something that resembled what I saw, I was determined to describe my own experience, to record what I was seeing. By taking notes and by tape-recording my conversations with people who were willing to let me experience their auras, I gained a sense of the organizational structure of the information that the colors represented. Over a period of four years, I compiled the information into the Personality Spectrums system. I have used this system to lead seminars on team building and communication skills for businesses and organizations, to consult on career development and employee placement, and to assist in executive recruitment. In my consulting practice, I have found that the system is valuable in developing communication skills within a group and between groups, because it helps people understand the different communication styles of the colors. In career development, I assist people in finding their unique niche, combining their innate capabilities with the career or job opportunity that best fits them. I work with executive recruiters in matching the applicant to the company with the employment fit most apt to work for the benefit of both.

As a result of the way the information is organized within the pattern of the aura, I have been able to develop a questionnaire that identifies the core personality and character traits manifested in the aura. The questionnaire is included in Chapter 2, along with a scoring key and an explanation of how to read the results. This questionnaire will tell you what color your aura is.

The balance of the book presents profiles of the fourteen Personality Spectrums colors that make up the system. These profiles are designed to give insight into individual styles of behavior and interaction.

The information in the Personality Spectrums profiles delineates the way people handle the major aspects of their lives. Each chapter is a detailed profile of each of the colors in the Personality Spectrums and is organized according to how that particular color works with the following aspects of an individual's life:

- *Approach to Physical Reality:* environment, health, and the real world
- *Mental Attitudes:* intellectual capabilities, thinking, and problem-solving skills
- *Emotional Makeup:* personal interactions and emotional health and well-being
- *Social Style:* friendships, intimate relationships
- *Compatibility with Other Colors:* strengths and weaknesses of each pair of colors for emotional, mental, and physical compatibility
- *Personal Power and Leadership Style:* power and leadership skills within a group

• *Financial Choices:* attitudes and values concerning money and finances
• *Career Options:* representative careers in which individual talents and capabilities would lead to success
• *Spirituality:* moral, ethical, and religious attitudes, feelings, and values*

The information in these nine main categories falls into definitive paradigms of thought and action. That means that each of the fourteen colors indicates unique ways of coping with the demands of life as they arise in these major areas. For example, each color has different ways of handling the needs and concerns of the real world. Some colors tackle the problems and literally wrestle them to the ground. Other colors will attempt to ignore problems, hoping that they will go away. As the entire range of potential behaviors in each of the nine areas is delineated, personality types emerge.

Each aura color has individual patterns of behavior that are distinct from each of the other colors. In some cases the behaviors may be similar, but the motivations that fuel those behaviors are different. For example, Yellows exercise because they have a difficult time sitting still. Mental Tans exercise because they think a fitness program is a good idea. Each aura color profile will describe the primary behavior patterns of individuals of that color. Understanding the basis of people's deep-seated drives helps us to be tolerant of the external actions or words of others.

The sections on compatibility are different for each aura color—how a Green relates to a Red may be different from how a Red relates to a Green. Therefore, you need to read in your color chapter how your color relates to your mate or lover, and then turn to your partner's color chapter to see how he or she relates to you. These sections on compatibility are not inclusive. They serve only to highlight the main issues

---

*For some Personality Spectrums colors, this spirituality is encompassed by the concept of a Higher Being, which I will refer to as "God." I use this term as a nondenominational reference. Spirituality sometimes, but not always, refers to a relationship with a Higher Being.

confronting the relationship. The section on compatibility can also be construed to include how one interacts with very close and intimate friends.

A word of caution: there are no "good" colors and no "bad" colors. Each color within the personality spectrum has strengths and weaknesses. The purpose of this system is to give people insights and tools for enhancing their strengths and to give them permission to turn to others to minimize their weaknesses. When people begin to understand that we all have our unique role and function in the order of the universe, they can concentrate on being the best they know how to be. If each of us concentrates on making our special contribution, no matter how small or insignificant it seems, the possibility of peace for our children becomes real.

The auric Personality Spectrums system provides a structure that can help people to identify, categorize, and comprehend their innate capabilities and talents. When individuals are able to focus their energies in the direction in which their soul-river is flowing, they are then able to identify opportunities that are uniquely theirs. This capability allows individuals to act with confidence, poise, and self-assurance. Therefore, by working with their innate skills and abilities, they maximize their opportunities for finding productive, satisfying work and loving, supportive relationships. When people work with their aura color, they give themselves the gift of personal peace, enhanced by a sense of personal fulfillment.

THE AURA

The aura is a luminous egg-shaped cloud of pulsing energy that surrounds the human body. It extends out from the body about six feet in all directions. It is made up of concentric bands or layers of colored light that travel in patterns around the body. To me, color is the most important aspect of the aura. Each color in the auric spectrum can vary greatly in hue and value. The more in touch we are with our own unique talents and skills, the richer, more luminous the colors in our aura will be. The colors of individuals who are emotionally withdrawn or have given up on life tend to fade into thin pastel washes. Good physical, mental, and emotional health is seen in clear, bright colors. Depression, anger, and self-pity tend to muddy the auric colors.

The aura is multidimensional. In addition to the molecules of colored light, the aura also has *size*. Some people's auras are large and full of information while others' are thin, indicating lives that are spiritually, mentally, and emotionally undernourished. The *shape* of the aura is indicative of the general health and well-being of an individual. It identifies areas of the body where an individual holds stress. The aura's *texture* is a result of the arrangement of the particles of light. A thick aura indicates the ability to search within oneself for information with which to solve problems. The aura also emits *patterns*, which are determined by the direction in which the molecules of light flow. These flow patterns indicate the general attitude an individual has toward life. An active pattern means that a person is engaging life in a healthy way. *Sound* is the high-pitched whine, or hum, that the aura emits. These six components combine to create a symbolic language which, when decoded, has provided the basis of the Personality Spectrums system.

I have found that the natural, rhythmic vibrations, which are the unique blueprint for each individual's life, are represented by the patterns of color and energy in the aura. The aura is the manifestation, or outpicturing, of an individual's feelings, values, and behavior patterns as well as attributes of character such as integrity, compassion, and trustworthiness. To understand the complexity of the aura is to understand the complexity of our own natures. This understanding allows us to tap into our reservoirs of personal power, autonomy, and spirituality. The better we know all aspects of ourselves, the better we can use our personal attributes to assist us in making decisions about our life.

For fifty years, Kirlian photography has been used to study the high-frequency energy fields known as the aura. The purpose has been to document the phenomenon of electromagnetic energy that emanates from all living organisms. Thelma Moss and Valerie Hunt of the University of California at Los Angeles have done extensive photographing of the aura using this process. Moss's research shows how the aura is represented by a blue flamelike glow emanating from the human body. When an individual is aroused in anger, this blue glow spits red sparks. When deep feelings of passion and love are being expressed by two individuals, the aura expands and changes color, and the two auras open to encompass each other, forming one elliptical aura.*

Kirlian photography does not pretend to prove the existence of the aura. It only points to evidence that something larger than just the physical form or body exists. Neither is Kirlian photography an accurate representation of the aura as I see it. These photographs represent the aura as a two-dimensional glow emanating from the perimeter of the body. The aura I see is a three-dimensional elliptical, or egg-shaped, cloud that is full of movement, light, and color.

In order to help explain how some individuals can see the aura, among other phenomena, the new field of neuropsychology has been developed to study the relationship between physiology, brain chemistry, and psychology. Leaders in the field, such as Robert Ornstein and Lawrence LeShan, have long postulated that there is much the brain can do which we do not yet have the science or technology to understand. However, we do have an increased understanding of left brain–right brain functioning and of the physical effects of prayer and meditation. This new knowledge, combined with advances in technology that allow us to record and photograph hitherto unseen realities, is bringing us closer to the ability to document the aura.

The aura is made up of many bands of color arranged in three layers. Each color has a separate and distinct meaning, and each layer addresses different life concerns and issues. For the purposes of this book, we will explore the band or bands closest to the body. These are the ones you were born with, the ones that contain the genetic makeup of your spiritual life force. They never vary during your normal life span.

_____

*Thelma Moss, *The Body Electric: A Personal Journey into the Mysteries of Parapsychological Research, Bioenergy, and Kirlian Photography* (Los Angeles: J. P. Tarcher, 1979), pp. 144–8.

The aura, as I see it, is a graphic representation of the human soul. It is not the soul, but an indicator of the soul; it is an external directional signal indicating the spiritual essence of the person wearing it. It is exquisitely beautiful; it is the outer proof of the magnificence of the human spirit.

Personality color bands are permanent. Their color changes only if an individual has undergone a *radical* life shift, usually precipitated by a life crisis such as extraordinary physical or psychological trauma. Physically, this means one must have had something similar to a near-death experience.

When I look at individuals, I immediately perceive a colored glow, or cast of light, all around them. It is as if they have been brushed lightly with a cloud of colored light, much the way an actor on stage is washed with colored light. The cloud of colored light is clear and distinct.

Remember that when I speak of seeing the aura, I mean that I see *rays* of light, *not* color pigmentation like the dyes and paints we use on our walls and clothing. All color theory is based on the principle that color is light. When a beam of white light passes through a prism, a spectrum of the entire range of pure colors visible to the human eye is formed. The color wheel associated with the spectrum of pure light has as its three primary colors violet-blue, orange-red, and green. (The color pigmentation wheel contains the primaries red, blue, and yellow.) The difference between the light spectrum and the pigmentation spectrum is the difference between a rainbow seen in the sky and a rainbow painted on a piece of paper.

The main color in your aura—your personality color—indicates your behavior and character style. As you become aware of your aura color, you can choose situations and actions that work for you, that are in harmony with your natural inclinations, that your brain and nervous sytem can handle most efficiently to bring you the most joy. Each color, with its attendant talents and abilities, has its own niche in the Personality Spectrums system.

THE COLOR OF LIGHT

There are fourteen Personality Spectrums colors within the auric spectrum that I see. Nine of these auras are named for colors as people usually see them: Red, Orange, Magenta, Yellow, Green, Blue, Violet, Lavender, and Indigo. I have given five further auras the names of special colors and combinations of colors that I see: Crystal, Mental Tan, Physical Tan, Nurturing Tan, and Loving Tan.

Mental Tan is best described as a rich golden honey color, and in the light spectrum it exists in the place where yellow-orange, yellow, and green coincide. I call this color Mental Tan to distinguish it from the double colors known as Physical Tan, Nurturing Tan, and Loving Tan.

Physical Tan, Nurturing Tan, and Loving Tan are so called because each represents *two* bands of color in the aura that encircles the body, and each is interpreted as *one* color. The band of color closest to the body is the one called Mental Tan. Then there is an eclipse, or a second ring of color, surrounding the body just outside the Mental Tan. In a Physical Tan, the tan band is surrounded with a band of green; Nurturing Tan is surrounded with a band of blue; and in a Loving Tan, the tan band is surrounded with a band of red. Each of these Personality Spectrums colors is unique and not a combination of the Mental Tan and Green, Blue, or Red.

Crystal, another of the unusual colors, has the appearance of an aurora borealis, or a rainbow shimmer, in the aura. Crystal does not represent the absence of color; it is a gossamer, foglike mist with other colors in it.

THE STRUCTURE OF THE PERSONALITY SPECTRUMS SYSTEM

The fourteen Personality Spectrums colors are organized into four families of colors. These four families determine the general way in which each group of colors relates to the environment. Each Personality Spectrums family of colors has either physical, mental, or emotional/spiritual strengths. The physical category is subdivided into two parts, indicating that some colors deal with life as an externalization of physicality, which other colors cope by internalizing within their physical bodies the signals and cues they receive from outer reality.

The four families are:

1. Physical (environment) Colors: Red, Orange, and Magenta
2. Physical (body) Colors: Yellow and Physical Tan
3. Mental Colors: Mental Tan, Green, Nurturing Tan, and Loving Tan
4. Emotional/Spiritual Colors: Blue, Violet, Lavender, Crystal, and Indigo

Colors within a family have a common way of expressing themselves. Those individuals whose colors are in the Physical Families—both those who express themselves through the external environment and those who communicate through their bodies—take their cues from the physical environment. Those in the Mental or Emotional/Spiritual Families tend to have an internal locus of control, basing their actions on thoughts and/or emotions.

The name given to each family group of colors indicates the dominant organizing principle by which these colors approach life and decision-making. Each color in the group approaches that organizing principle in a different way.

The organizing principle of the Physical (environment) Family of colors is that they relate to the world by interacting with their physical environment. They understand who they are and what their place in the world is through their physical interaction with it. Their reality is tangible; they need to see, hear, feel, and handle ideas in the form of tangible products or physical experiences. These colors require manifestation. For them, that means "making it happen." These colors live life with gusto, verve, and courage.

On the other hand, those who are in the Physical (body) Family of colors relate to the world through the sensations triggered by the biochemistry of their physical bodies. They get their bearings in the world by placing themselves within a three-dimensional reality, unlike those in the Physical (environment) Family, who must push up against reality. The

Physical (body) colors translate human dynamics into bio-chemical reactions within their bodies which they then experience as a fight/flight syndrome, gut reactions, and nervousness that translates into fidgeting. The command center for the Physical (body) Family of colors is the solar plexus. These colors are more kinesthetic than other colors and as such must learn to listen to the cues they get through their physical body.

Those in the Mental Family of colors (Mental Tan, Green, Nurturing Tan, and Loving Tan) *think* about the world and their place in it. Their primary process is cerebral. They are logical thinkers who see everything in their reality as an idea. They love to play with ideas and organizing systems. They are happiest when they are able to mentally grasp and manipulate the environment through the realm of ideas. Their biggest challenge is trying to deal with their emotions logically.

The five colors in the Emotional/Spiritual Family—Blue, Violet, Lavender, Crystal, and Indigo—all live in a world where the intangibles of life such as hopes, wishes, and dreams are more important than the tangibles. Emotions and feelings are the coin of their realm. These colors are happiest, most productive, and creative when they are interacting through their intuitive and emotional faculties rather than through their mental faculties. Abstraction has more reality to them than does paying the bills.

There is an interrelationship of strengths, capabilities, and talents in the structure of the color families. The Physical (environment) Families and the Physical (body) Families both deal with tangible reality; they are present in the here and now, not in the past or in future abstractions. Mental and Emotional/Spiritual Families are both concerned with intangible reality, but the Mental Family of colors focuses on ideas, while the Emotional/Spiritual Family is primarily concerned with envisioning the future.

In addition, the individual Personality Spectrums colors arrange themselves according to whether they are more concerned with product or process. This means that some colors must create, produce, develop, or manufacture some sort of tangible product as a result of their endeavors. Other colors

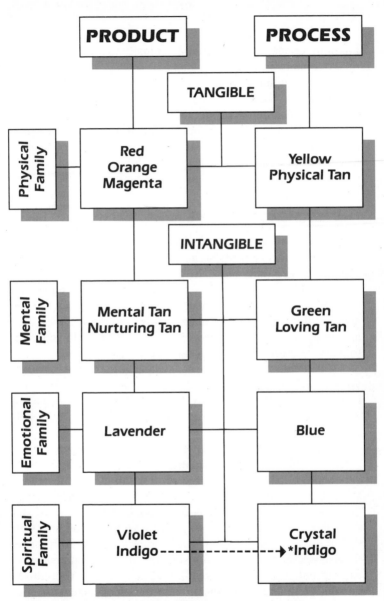

PRODUCT		PROCESS
	TANGIBLE	
Physical Family	Red Orange Magenta	Yellow Physical Tan
	INTANGIBLE	
Mental Family	Mental Tan Nurturing Tan	Green Loving Tan
Emotional Family	Lavender	Blue
Spiritual Family	Violet Indigo - - - - - - - - →	Crystal →*Indigo

*INDIGOS START AS PRODUCT AND GRADUALLY, THROUGH THEIR LIFETIMES, MOVE INTO PROCESS.

21

are more concerned with the way something is done than with its outcome or result.

As individuals begin to work with the information contained within the Personality Spectrums system, a language for communicating and appreciating capabilities and talents of other personality types will be developed. Once members of a family or team at work know their basic interaction style, they can begin to cooperate with the strengths of other team and family members, thereby enhancing the efforts of all.

THE PSYCHOLOGY OF THE AURA

This book presents an organizational system that describes personality traits so as to create a practical means of gaining insight into the self. Familiarity with the fourteen colors within the Personality Spectrums system will allow you to build a foundation for understanding the complexity of the many different ways of being. This system will help you appreciate your own unique skills and abilities while you learn to work with others' special skills and abilities.

The Personality Spectrums system is designed to guide you toward a clearer understanding of what it means to have a healthy, or well, personality. The patterns of information within the aura represent a system that has as its goal self-actualization.

The aura is not reflective of socialization or parenting patterns. This means that the aura does not reflect the parents' expectations of the child's future. The aura indicates those skills, talents, and proclivities a child is born with. The aura is the external indicator of the potentiality within one's soul. Too often parents attempt to overlay their own frustrated hopes on their children instead of allowing their children to express themselves authentically, choosing activities and interests that emerge out of their own growth and need cycle. The educational system and the media attempt to homogenize us so that we "forget" who we are. Some people know they are scientists, happy and productive in an environment that supports the logical, linear thinking process that is so necessary to that discipline. To force that linear thinking pattern on an individual who solves problems in a holographic way would be to create job stress and burnout, leading to a lowered sense of self-esteem and self-worth. By understanding the individual strengths within each color in the auric system, you can avoid this problem by allowing the flourishing of a child's unique talents and abilities.

The chapters that follow describe the *idiosyncratic behavior* of each personality type. We all have quirks, habits, and patterns that are unique to the color of our personality. The aura is a code that determines how we grapple with the main issues of our lives. We all have strengths and weaknesses. What we need is a way to discover our "best self," and not to envy the strengths and potentials of others. The aura encompasses healthy traits and affirms our individuality. It can become the tool to help us understand our own complex natures.

I have written this book in the hope that it will give you a new insight into yourself. This is not a short course in psychotherapy or a prescription for health or fulfillment. Nor is it the last word on auras or on personality types. It is simply a report of my observations about people's behavior over a period of years. It is a system that my clients have found useful.

In the five years I have been using this system, people all over the country have consistently reported that they have found benefit and value in it. It is a system that accentuates the positive while pointing out those behaviors that are counterproductive to good mental health. The system is practical, it makes sense, and it has applications that cross cultural, economic, and educational differences.

I am making no claims that by using this system you will develop good mental health or achieve emotional fulfillment. However, if you gain some small insight into yourself, then I am glad that the information has proved beneficial and valuable. Fill out the questionnaire. Find out what Personality Spectrum color you are, and then make up your own mind as to the validity of the information.

The most important issue in a person's life is the relationship of the self to the Self, that inner sanctum of one's soul or heart. The world is full of ideas and techniques designed to give insight and perspective into the attitudes and values that influence decisions and behavior. These various processes give individuals an opportunity to sort through multiple ways of acting and being—to say, "This is me; this is not me." The purpose of any growth path is to find what is authentic and real about one's self. The information encoded within one's aura is a shortcut through this process; the Personality Spectrums system gives one the tools to understand oneself and others.

The aura is a visual, symbolic structure that can provide you with a great deal of information about yourself. It becomes a framework for understanding your relationships, careers, spirituality, leadership roles, and physical and mental processes. In addition, it provides specific tools, insights, and awarenesses that allows you to make concrete, positive changes in life. The aura is your key to partnership with yourself. When you are functioning in ways that are true to yourself, life becomes exciting, the world becomes a friendly place in which to live. To be in partnership with your Self is the first step toward becoming a co-Creator with God, becoming a change-agent for the future, and living life with enthusiasm.

TWO

THE QUESTIONNAIRE

As the Personality Spectrums system began to evolve, people kept asking me how they could use the system if they could not see the auras.

Since that was a legitimate question, I gave it a great deal of thought. About the same time, I noticed that many of my friends could correctly identify individuals' aura color, even though I knew they could not see the aura as I do. Because my system is based on personality patterns and internal psychological structures, the information lends itself to the development of a test instrument.

The purpose of the questionnaire is to begin to make the information within the aura more accessible to people. After you fill in the questionnaire, you will be on your way to opening the door to a new way of looking at yourself and gaining insight into and understanding of your life.

The questionnaire that follows is designed to identify your primary aura color, the band of color closest to your body, which contains the predominant character and behavior traits that distinguish your personality. This band will be indicated by the group of questions in which you score the highest number of points (35 being the maximum number).

We are all "rainbows of colors." At different times in our lives, we give priority to different needs and wants. On the questionnaire, most of you will score relatively high on at least two colors. The secondary score—that is, the aura color in which you have the second highest score—is your *overlay,* the second band of color in the aura that radiates out around your head and shoulders like a halo, outside the primary color. The overlay represents a secondary group of attributes that are available for you to draw on. (An overlay is different from an eclipse, which is a full band of green, red, or blue attached to the tan color.) Usually we are willing to try on new behaviors and attempt new challenges at times when we feel good about ourselves. The overlay process is one of adding to—not replacing—the qualities and capabilities inherent in your Personality Spectrums color. (Some of you may find you have only one significantly high score. In that case, you do not have an overlay of note.)

As you fill in the questionnaire you may find that the qualities within your primary color seem to be antithetical to your overlay. We all have parts of ourselves that seem incongruous with other parts. Having both positive and negative tendencies within the same psyche causes some people to be in constant conflict with themselves. Awareness of your primary color and your overlay color will give you an opportunity to be aware of these conflicts within yourself and to work at learning how to deal with them.

Your primary Personality Spectrums color is the most dominant pattern in your aura. No matter what other colors your aura contains, when placed under stress you revert to those behaviors that are inherent to this main aura color. However, when you feel good about yourself, because you have achieved a goal, taken a successful risk, or been successful in a new endeavor, then you are willing to attempt new attitudes and change your behavior. Those are the times when your overlay comes into play. Problems occur when individuals are reluctant to move beyond their personal comfort zones (the primary color) and experiment with the overlay attributes. Your overlay can be your open door to enrichment and vitality because it represents the abilities and talents of your growing personality.

In answering the questions on the personality profile instrument, it is very important for you to be honest with yourself. Here are some guidelines for doing this questionnaire:

- Carefully read the five "key" answers.
- Make a determination in your mind as to what the words *seldom, sometimes,* and *often* mean to you.
- Take the test once, quickly. Fill in the number corresponding to your "key" answer adjacent to the question.
- Put down the first answer that comes to your mind.
- If you have difficulty with a question, this is probably an attribute or trait that is *least* like you.
- If no quick answer comes to mind, leave the item blank and come back to it after you have finished the rest of the questionnaire.
- Go through the questionnaire the first time without stopping to analyze every response in detail; just put down what feels right at first.

When you have completed the test, run a trial score. (See instructions on scoring on page 29.) Find the colors in which you have scored the highest; then go back and reread those questions, considering each answer much more carefully. Answer these questions again and compute your new score. The score you get this second time will reflect your true personality.

If you find that you are giving yourself many 4s and 5s, or if you have high scores in three or more of the color categories, you are probably not being as careful and truthful as you could be in your answers. If you score 25 to 30 points on three or more colors, carefully retake those sections of the questionnaire. Go back over the questionnaire and try again, paying strict attention to the shades of meaning between the different numbers used in the scoring system. Three high scores indicate that you are probably trying to be all things to all people. The benefit in this system is that you get to be yourself.

Should you get two identical high scores, your overlay and primary color are nearly the same intensity. This indicates a need to look at who you are authentically as opposed to who you are after you have developed coping mechanisms within your personality structure. Many of us have learned to be and do things that don't come naturally to us in order to cope and succeed in the world we live in. Consider these issues closely, and answer the questionnaire according to your true self, your personality before you adapted and modified it.

If you score a high secondary score as a red overlay, be aware that this color has special meanings which are discussed at the end of the chapter on Reds.

It is important to remember that no aura color is better than any other color. Therefore, there are no right or wrong answers. The purpose of this exercise is to help you identify your aura color and the personality characteristics that go with each color.

Since we all have the potential to be a rainbow of colored light, it is theoretically possible for you to get significantly different scores if you take the test at different times in your life. However, most of us have a core set of behaviors that form a consistent pattern in our lives.

Each color indicates a mode of being; we can all access behavior patterns from different modes. For example, Blues are intuitive thinkers who seem to pull ideas and concepts out of thin air. However, when it is demanded of them, they can be as methodical, linear, and sequential in their thinking as any Mental Tan. The difference is that while this more strictly logical approach is easy and elegant for a Mental Tan, it is frustrating for a Blue. While we describe ourselves as being predominantly either left-brained or right-brained, we all use both mental processes. It is just that some of us use one side of the brain more consistently than the other. Similarly, your aura indicates your primary modes of behavior, not your sole personality potentials.

This questionnaire serves to evaluate the order of your bands of color. You might use three or four different modes equally.

Instructions

- There are 98 short statements in this test.
- Don't try to read hidden meaning into them.
- First, take the test quickly. Record your first reaction to the statement as it best describes you.

● Use the "key" to evaluate your answer and record the appropriate number value next to the question.

● Answer each statement with a number from 1 to 5:

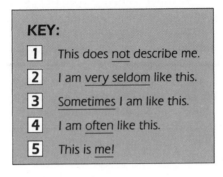

KEY:

1	This does <u>not</u> describe me.
2	I am <u>very seldom</u> like this.
3	<u>Sometimes</u> I am like this.
4	I am <u>often</u> like this.
5	This is <u>me</u>!

Scoring

A sample score sheet follows the test. Several additional scoring sheets can be found at the back of the book. Some of you may want to remove these to use them.

1. After you finish the test, record the answers on the score sheet. You will fill in your answers in chronological order, working from top to bottom on the score sheet.

2. After you have entered your score for each statement on the score sheet, fold the page along the dotted line on the right-hand side. Match up each row with its corresponding "total" box. Use the heavy ruled horizontal lines to help fold the sheet correctly.

3. After you have folded the sheet, add up the scores for each row from left to right and record each in the appropriate box.

4. Once you have recorded your totals, unfold the sheet and turn it over. Your totals on the back side of the score sheet will correspond to an aura color designation. These scores will indicate your aura color and family of colors.

If you have several high scores clustered in one family of colors, such as the Mental Family, you have identified your primary function or style of being. Now go back and carefully review the questions for those colors. This will assist you in differentiating your unique individual process. If you have high scores scattered among all the families, you have many socialization patterns. In other words, you do things to please others and not yourself. Go back and find the group of questions that is most representative of what you truly believe about yourself, about the person you were before you adapted to your environment.

You may want to give friends and family an opportunity to take the questionnaire. This way you can share this system with others while at the same time giving you insight as to how you can improve communications patterns with them. It might also be fun to see how you score others as opposed to how they score themselves.

KEY:

1   This does not describe me.

2   I am very seldom like this.

3   Sometimes I am like this.

4   I am often like this.

5   This is me!

THE QUESTIONNAIRE

1 You are methodical in your thinking.

2 You have a strong inner desire to make your mark on the world.

3 You resent emotional and domestic demands made on you.

4 Esoteric spiritual or political philosophies have great emotional and intellectual appeal for you.

5 You seek the unusual or the avant-garde.

6 You cry easily.

7 You are not judgmental or critical of the ways in which others express their emotions or feelings.

8 You are at ease in any environment where healing is the primary activity or occupation.

9 When faced with a dangerous task, you carefully plan how to handle any crisis that may arise.

10 You are a loner.

11 When solving problems, you are able to visualize all the steps and the solution at the same time.

12 You have no biases about sexuality—heterosexuality, bisexuality, or homosexuality.

13 You prefer working at jobs that are physically demanding.

14 You react physically (with sweaty palms, for example) before you respond to a situation mentally or emotionally.

15 As a leader, you solicit lots of detailed information from others in order to make decisions.

16 Social get-togethers such as cocktail parties bore you.

17 You prefer occupations that have unlimited financial opportunity, such as sales.

18 When you have money, you spend it; when you don't, you don't.

19 You are a nonconformist.

20 You have a hard time saying no when people ask you to do them a favor.

21 You organize projects by creating systems.

22 You depend on other people for clues on how you should act in various social situations.

23 You meet physical challenges without fear.

24 You are slow to choose friends.

25 You do not require emotional loyalty to effectively mentor someone.

26 In school, you learn most effectively in an unstructured environment.

27 For you, sex is for physical pleasure.

28 When you find yourself in a tense situation, you want to run away or pretend it does not exist.

29 You have difficulty sharing your emotions and feelings with others.

30 You would rather be the theorist of a project, and leave the building of the working model to someone else.

31 You diagnose problems by recognizing patterns.

32 You are a dreamer who likes to live in the fantasies you create.

KEY:

1 This does not describe me.

2 I am very seldom like this.

3 Sometimes I am like this.

4 I am often like this.

5 This is me!

33 You are a spontaneous person.

34 The experience of God's love is the spiritual force in your life.

35 You look for ways to improve your community.

36 You rarely show your deepest feelings.

37 You prefer activities that allow you to demonstrate physical prowess.

38 You evaluate objects by how solid or substantial they feel.

39 You are attracted to religions with strong theological structures that allow for personal interpretation.

40 You lead by forcing others to rethink and reexamine old beliefs, values, and ways of doing things.

41 When you lose your temper, you get over it quickly.

42 You are not cynical.

43 You like social activities that combine business and pleasure.

44 You are not "free and easy" when spending your money on others.

45 You see God as the "brain" that created the universe.

46 You express your sexuality creatively, intuitively, and experimentally.

47 You are attracted to products that have unusual or unexpected design features.

48 When looking for a job, you have difficulty asking for the salary you deserve.

49 You feel that raising a well-educated child is the greatest contribution you can make to your community.

50 You enjoy reading biographies and diaries that describe the lives of real people.

51 You prefer individual competition rather than team effort.

52 You are slow to commit to any belief system.

53 You eagerly seek to please those you love and care about.

54 You perceive spirituality to be in everything you do.

55 If you have enough money to buy the necessities, you are happy.

56 You experience God as the physical sensation of the joy of being alive.

57 You prefer a spiritual belief system that relies on a foundation of laws and principles.

58 You lead by telling people what to do.

59 You prefer a few specially chosen friends who stimulate you intellectually.

60 Your artistic pursuits often keep you indoors.

61 You form loose friendships that are not encumbered with bonds of expectation.

62 You feel more comfortable sharing the leadership by being a co-chairperson.

63 You financially support community groups and programs that benefit society.

64 Your source of personal power is your ability to mentally retreat inward.

65 You are not interested in organized religion or other belief systems.

66 You are meticulous in following instructions given to you by your supervisor.

KEY:

1 This does not describe me.

2 I am very seldom like this.

3 Sometimes I am like this.

4 I am often like this.

5 This is me!

67 You prefer social gatherings where you have an opportunity to talk to many different people.

68 You need to be awakened slowly from a sound sleep to avoid being irritable or in physical pain.

69 When playing a team sport, you rally the team when the chips are down.

70 You like parties.

71 To you, money is security.

72 You feel compelled to do something significant with your life.

73 You find great satisfaction in assisting people by giving ideas and information.

74 You prefer a somewhat isolated existence rather than one in which you would have to conform to society's expectations.

75 When you see something that you like, you choose to have your fantasy now and pay later.

76 You do not enjoy endurance sports such as cross-country skiing or weight-lifting.

77 You feel that spiritual principles must have practical application in the real world.

78 You prefer quiet, introspective, spiritual disciplines.

79 You prefer to work for a commission, or even as a freelancer, rather than for a regular, fixed salary.

80 You believe that to be a good leader, you must first be a good follower.

81 You have difficulty managing money effectively.

82 You cannot be coerced into doing something in which you are not interested.

83 You experience spirituality when you physically participate in the worship service.

84 You lead others with enthusiasm because you enjoy being with people.

85 You enjoy working with mechanical devices such as computers, calculators, and stereo equipment.

86 Possessions are important to you as stepping-stones to power and influence.

87 To you, ideas are things, not mental abstractions.

88 You see ideas as three-dimensional patterns.

89 You express your spirituality through your strong connection with nature.

90 When making a decision, you try to find a solution that will please everyone.

91 You lead others by incorporating their feelings into the decision-making process.

92 You work best in an environment that is calm and peaceful with limited contact with others.

93 You do not need friends or social interaction to be happy.

94 To you, money represents physical safety and stability.

95 You have difficulty keeping track of personal possessions.

96 You are content to work with your hands.

97 You want to know how and why things work the way they do.

98 You enjoy working in occupations that require physical activity.

KEY:

1 This does not describe me.

2 I am very seldom like this.

3 Sometimes I am like this.

4 I am often like this.

5 This is me!

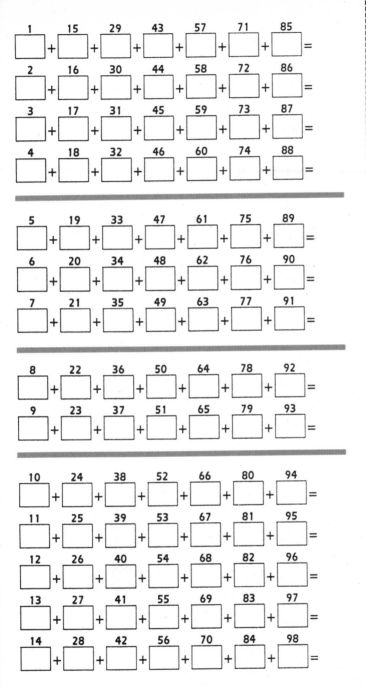

1 + 15 + 29 + 43 + 57 + 71 + 85 =

2 + 16 + 30 + 44 + 58 + 72 + 86 =

3 + 17 + 31 + 45 + 59 + 73 + 87 =

4 + 18 + 32 + 46 + 60 + 74 + 88 =

5 + 19 + 33 + 47 + 61 + 75 + 89 =

6 + 20 + 34 + 48 + 62 + 76 + 90 =

7 + 21 + 35 + 49 + 63 + 77 + 91 =

8 + 22 + 36 + 50 + 64 + 78 + 92 =

9 + 23 + 37 + 51 + 65 + 79 + 93 =

10 + 24 + 38 + 52 + 66 + 80 + 94 =

11 + 25 + 39 + 53 + 67 + 81 + 95 =

12 + 26 + 40 + 54 + 68 + 82 + 96 =

13 + 27 + 41 + 55 + 69 + 83 + 97 =

14 + 28 + 42 + 56 + 70 + 84 + 98 =

FOLD

TOTAL
MENTAL TAN

TOTAL
VIOLET

TOTAL
GREEN

TOTAL
LAVENDER

TOTAL
MAGENTA

TOTAL
BLUE

TOTAL
NURTURING TAN

TOTAL
CRYSTAL

TOTAL
ORANGE

TOTAL
PHYSICAL TAN

TOTAL
LOVING TAN

TOTAL
INDIGO

TOTAL
RED

TOTAL
YELLOW

38

THREE

RED

Physical and sexual expression is the hallmark of a Red. The key to success for Reds is to act on what they know about physical reality and the tangible environment. Reds are literal in their interpretation of what goes on around them. They are not abstract thinkers; for them a table is a table, period. They are comfortable and safe in the world of nature and the elements. They pursue life with gusto, verve, and courage.

The most powerful aspect of Reds is their ability to be in the world, to manage the aspects and realities of everyday living with self-confidence and assurance. Their gift is the respect and awe they have for the majesty and might of nature. They seem to understand their role in the equation of humans and physical reality. Whether they are riding out a hurricane, rescuing a person from a burning building, or living their own lives, Reds love being here.

APPROACH TO PHYSICAL REALITY

Reds identify with the world by interacting with the physical environment. They understand who they are by rearranging furniture. They love the challenge of manipulating mass and weight. Individuals of this Personality Spectrums color feel *alive,* comfortable with themselves, powerful and in charge when they are able to relate in a physical way. Their reality is tangible; if they can see, hear, taste, touch, and smell it, then it is real. They are literal in their interpretation of the

39

world. Reds require manifestation—proof that ideas have substance.

Reds love to subdue their environment. For them, reality is a physical challenge, one they are overjoyed to meet. To exist in relation with objects gives Reds a sense of definition; they need specific physical parameters within the context of time and space. Consequently, Reds frequently find themselves in situations demanding physical exertion, strength, and stamina. Moving furniture, unloading cargo, or putting out fires gives them an opportunity to test their intrepidity. They prefer a physical challenge to a mental or emotional one.

In a society that increasingly relies on machines to do the labor of Reds, the tangible contribution of this aura color often goes unnoticed and unappreciated. Reds cheerfully accept the physical labor necessary to make even the smallest events happen. When it comes time to set up and take down, Reds are eager and willing to assist. Loading and unloading boxes of supplies, moving items from one place to another, and setting up displays are activities that give Reds a sense of purpose and a reason for being. This assures them of a place in any organizational structure. Reds are intelligent and capable of contributing ideas, but unless they have some proof of tangibility, an idea remains, to them, nebulous and ungrounded. It is the Reds' purpose in life to give substance to the ideas, emotions, and desires of others.

Reds are here to remind us that we have a physical body, that we are matter to which have been added intellect, emotions, and spirituality. Reds remind us that the body is the structure that houses all the other parts of ourselves. Reds would not wish away the physicalness of their being, as the Emotional/Spiritual Families tend to do.

Reds are the rugged individualists of the spectrum. Once they have decided on a course of action, they will stay with it until the end. They do not listen to a different drummer so much as they listen to their own instincts. They take their cues from the weather; they automatically read the danger involved or the risk factor. They have a certain animal wariness and cunning for survival. As firemen or other rescue personnel, they have a sense of being able to control physical elements, bringing human life safely through danger. In the field of disaster preparedness, they instinctively know what attitudes, resources, and skills will help people survive a crisis such as a flood, fire, earthquake, or war.

MENTAL ATTITUDES

Red is the practical Personality Spectrums color. These individuals deal with the exigencies of reality. They are down-to-earth, unafraid of hard work, and more patient with tasks that require practical application skills than are those in the Mental or Emotional/Spiritual Families of colors. Because they feel the need to make something happen, Reds do not do well in situations wherein they are forced to wait for something to develop. They prefer an offensive position to a defensive one.

Reds often choose occupations and interests that allow them to assume a certain mastery over their own time, resources, and energy. They often go into business for themselves in order to be their own boss. If they own a repair garage, they always have more work than they can accomplish in one day so that they never have downtime waiting for parts to come in. This gives them a feeling of freedom and independence.

In their mental process, Reds try to figure out what makes the world tick. They have little patience with abstractions; they prefer school subjects that have practical application to strictly theoretical courses. They do better in wood shop than in art appreciation. Reds are curious and inquisitive. As children, they poke anthills to see what will happen, or take apart lawn mowers to find out how they work. However, their tolerance level for frustration is low. In this country's current educational system, Reds have difficulty staying in step with everyone else. They need physical latitude to take what they learn and apply it. Theory alone does not find a comfortable resting place in the minds of Reds. They must not only know why something works but also how it works and for what purpose it exists. They do not have great patience with long-term cause/effect relationships. Their question is: How will this theory, principle, or knowledge serve me *now?*

Reds excel at dealing with tactile reality—anything having weight, density, and specific gravity. They tend to choose occupations that fill the physical needs of a community; thus, they may become automobile mechanics, butchers, or heavy-equipment operators. These occupations represent the reality of life, as opposed to occupations that deal with abstractions, such as philosophy or theoretical science. Reds love seeing immediate results of their work or ideas. They are action oriented and often jump the gun in their eagerness to be doing something. They require activities that channel and direct their energies. An ideal job for a Red will be specific, will have definite goals and measurable behavioral objectives, will require manual dexterity and physical stamina, and will offer an opportunity for personal performance as well as team or group dynamics. Loading a moving van, pruning trees, and playing defensive line for a football team are among the activities that give Reds specific, concrete information to work with. Either all the furniture gets put on the van or it doesn't. Either the team wins the game or it doesn't. When confronted with too much furniture and not enough van, the options are simple and clear-cut to a Red: unload and order a bigger van; leave some possessions behind; or find another way to transport the left-overs. When a decision has been reached, a Red is propelled into action. Reds understand *action*.

In business and industry, Reds are an indispensable unit of the team because they have the know-how to make things happen, to get concepts into production and ideas off the drawing boards. Reds do not like to sit in planning meetings all day. Give them an idea and they will return with prices, options, alternatives, and production schedules. They will have located suppliers, manufacturers, and distributors. To them, an idea left floating in the air is useless. Therefore, they want to put a floor under that idea as soon as possible. To Reds, an idea is no good until it has been moved out of the realm of the theoretical into the realm of the physical.

EMOTIONAL MAKEUP

Emotionally, Reds are forthright and honest in expressing their emotions; they do so without guile or manipulation. They are eager, hopeful, dauntless, and expectant in *every situation*. They anticipate the best. Only after much frustration and disappointment will they concede defeat, experience loss and sadness, and finally abandon their hoped-for outcomes. However, they are quick to recover from disappointment and to re-ignite the spark of hope and eagerness. They are able to remain emotionally stable despite a wide range of fluctuating feelings because they are physically strong. They can withstand the emotional vicissitudes of others because they are so connected to physical reality.

This behavior is not to be confused with naiveté or a Pollyanna attitude. Reds are practical. They are strong, confident, and unflappable. Their greatest assets are their courage, honesty, and trustworthiness. Because of their fortitude in the face of defeat, they are capable of keeping hope alive in others. Since they are honest with themselves and others, they confront obstacles head on, intent on wresting success from defeat. A Red is often the spark plug of the team, the one who refuses to give up, thereby preserving dignity so that rebuilding can take place. Reds are able to evaluate what has been gained, even when confronted with losses.

The greatest emotional liability for Reds is their explosive temper. When confronted with emotional frustration that has no appropriate outlet, a Red will seek release in one of two ways: through intense sexual activity or by striking out physically. When confronted with a situation that has no resolution, Reds want to break the place up. Reds are slow to anger, but once aroused, they express their rage quickly. They never hold a grudge, however. Once expressed, their anger vanishes; they quickly forget the cause of their emotional fireworks. However, when they experience such strong feelings, mentally healthy and socially responsible Reds will find appropriate outlets for their anger and frustration. Anger and rage left to fester within a Red's personality may require professional psychotherapeutic intervention.

SOCIAL STYLE

Reds love and need other people in their lives. However, experience has taught them a certain wariness. While they need the interaction and companionship of friends and loved ones, they are vulnerable to emotional pain because they do not have the words or the mental concepts to express what goes on inside them. When hurt emotionally, they are like animals who express their pain in physical ways. Therefore, when dealing with such traumas as abandonment, betrayal, or rejection, Reds might throw dishes, put a fist through a wall, or walk out and slam the door. They find it hard not to take their hurt and frustration out on other people, and they are likely to lash out physically to assuage their own emotional pain. Because Reds are aware of this potential for physical violence within themselves, they are slow to be open and trusting in relationships. They have difficulty expressing what they are experiencing physically and what they are feeling emotionally. To protect themselves, they always seem to hold a part of themselves apart. This distancing, if not understood by friends and mates, can cause hurt feelings and even further emotional withdrawal.

Socially, Reds tend to stay at the fringes of parties and get-togethers, never becoming a part of the crowd. They tend to circle an activity or a group, joining it when they feel comfortable or when a niche has been created for them. Reds need to preserve a physical zone of safety, one they can withdraw to when they become overwhelmed by the complexities of life and society. It is difficult for others to comprehend the Reds' physical exuberance followed by emotional withdrawal, but this is the Reds' way of balancing their physical needs against their emotional needs. In attempting to find and maintain this balance, Reds vacillate between rowdy good times and long periods of isolation. They use their time alone to create and maintain equilibrium within themselves.

For most other Personality Spectrums colors, sexuality is primarily an emotional experience; for a Red, however, sexuality is life itself. Reds express their emotions through their carnal bodies. This Personality Spectrums color has an enthusiastic lust for life; Reds live with gusto, embracing everything life has to offer. They are sexual, grabbing at experiences and sensations, savoring them to the fullest.

Because Reds are so physical, they have difficulty understanding the moral strictures our society places on sexual behavior. For them sex represents fun, play, and enjoyable body sensations. Sexual release is not always about love, devotion, or tenderness. To a Red, it is often just about physicality, animal instincts, lust. They do not see life, the procreative act of life, as "dirty." To them it is the most natural expression of life. Sexual activity is a splendid opportunity for Reds to be joyful. For a Red, the moment of orgasmic climax is equivalent to a spiritual experience for other colors. Reds know the thrill of awe and wonder at the magnificence of the sexual experience; it allows them to access an aspect of God and oneness with the universe. A Red has an innate understanding of the ancient ceremonies and celebrations that revolved around the act of procreation as a symbolic representation of man's and woman's connection to the Divine and a reaffirmation of the God-self.

COMPATIBILITY WITH OTHER COLORS

Physical (environmental) Colors

Reds mated to any of the Physical (environmental) Colors—Red, Orange, or Magenta—can experience conflicts. These Personality Spectrums colors are fiercely independent and carefully guard the inner citadel of their feelings. Therefore, while there can be a great deal of lusty, exciting physical sexual expression between Reds and Physical Family colors, there is little intimacy. As a result, these relationships resemble volatile chemical compounds. They're apt to blow apart with very little agitation.

Reds mated to Reds will have the same inherent strengths and weaknesses. Both partners will be driven to tell the truth, which in its unvarnished form can cause pain and anger. Because Reds have difficulty relating to their feelings, they can find themselves walled off in this sort of relationship.

Both Oranges and Reds tend to be loners, and both need plenty of time alone. Both of these aura colors tend to be the silent type, possessing few skills for communicating their needs. As a result, it would be difficult for them to live together comfortably unless they had different work schedules.

Magentas push everything to the limit—clothing, hair styles, life-style. A Red often describes a Magenta's taste as bizarre instead of avant-garde. A Red would find a Magenta's rhythm and schedule too unpredictable to feel stability within the relationship.

Physical (body) Colors

Yellows bring a level of playfulness and uninhibited joy into a relationship with a Red. The sexual union between these two colors is dynamic and powerful. Because both colors tend to live in the "now" moment, joint financial security can be a problem. However, they both love to work, have a lot of friends, and always know how to keep a roof over their head and food in their stomachs.

Physical Tans and Reds can both be strong, silent types. However, they have many traits that balance well. Neither likes to be hemmed in, but both are loyal and trustworthy in a committed relationship. They form a tight partnership.

Mental Colors

Mental Tans are logical, steady, and security conscious; Reds are independent, hardworking, and, on occasion, volatile. The physicality of the Reds helps the Mental Tans get out of their head, and the intellectual capabilities of a Mental Tan give balance and structure to a Red's energy, assisting the Red in creating positive outlets for self-expression.

Greens—with their agile, creative minds that leap and frolic in information—are a wonder and a fascination for Reds, who never tire of the speed with which a Green can process data. Reds, with their uninhibited sexual expression, arouse the latent sensuality of the Green. Couples with this combination generate a lot of good ideas and then have the physical energy to put them into action.

Nurturing Tans tend to be too polite, gracious, and proper for Reds. Nurturing Tans are so self-effacing that a Red finds little challenge in the relationship.

Loving Tans with their random thinking process are too

scattered for a Red. The Loving Tan usually has a myriad of details always up in the air. This makes a Red feel ungrounded and unsafe. However, the Red appreciates the deep sense of compassion that Loving Tans bring to any relationship, providing acceptance and understanding for the Red's way of relating.

Emotional/Spiritual Colors

Blues and Reds are an oil-and-water combination. Blues are emotional and physically passive; they gain enjoyment from quiet activities such as reading and writing. On the other hand, Reds are physically active and emotionally unavailable to develop the deep, feeling level of spiritual communion that a Blue wants and desires in a relationship. A Blue wants to know what a Red is thinking and feeling, and the Red thinks it is none of the Blue's business.

Violets and Reds seem to know and understand one another even though they are essentially at the opposite ends of the Personality Spectrums. Violets are largely intuitive, and Reds are primarily physical. However, Violets recognize that many of their concepts will never be more than good ideas without the Reds' capabilities to implement them. Violets and Reds can create a dynamic duo once they understand that the process works because they both have something of equal value to bring to the relationship.

Lavenders refuse to be tied down either emotionally or physically. They can be like Tinker Bell, appearing and disappearing at will. Reds see this behavior as irresponsible and undependable. Reds like being able to count on their partner to hold up their end of the relationship. The sheer physical force and power of the Reds' color causes Lavenders to escape into their fantasy dream world.

Crystals find the power of the Red too overwhelming. However, Crystals admire the groundedness of a Red and may draw on that energy to anchor themselves. Reds resent this taking of their energy and usually give Crystals a wide berth.

Indigos and Reds have so little in common that a relationship between them is not propitious.

CAREER OPTIONS

Reds are ideally suited to any vocation that allows them to spend long periods of time alone engaged in physically demanding work, followed by a period of camaraderie and rowdy fellowship. Life as a Great Plains cowboy, which included long days alone on the trail broken by binges at the railhead towns, was ideal for a Red.

Reds want to make things happen. When their energy is channeled appropriately, many Reds discover their finest hour during times of disaster and war—when their pent-up frustrations are worked out in feats of strength, determination, and courage. Acts of heroism that call for this form of motivational anger can provide Reds with appropriate outlets for their sense of rage and helplessness.

Reds love working with their hands and are not afraid to get dirty. Men and women Reds alike love occupations that put them in charge of, or in competition with, their environment. Occupations that involve the use or repair of heavy machinery, or any jobs where they are actively engaged with the environment, give a Red a sense of making things happen.

Reds enjoy working as engineers (mechanical or civil), construction crew members (especially heavy equipment operators and repairmen), surgeons, physical therapists, police officers, fire fighters, paramedics, cocktail waitresses, bartenders, athletes (especially football players and weight lifters), shop foremen, and production supervisors.

SPIRITUALITY

Spirituality is a difficult concept for this Personality Spectrums color. Reds need positive proof of the intangibles of life, such as one's relationship with God. This color requires _action_, a sense of doing-ness, a feeling that they have a part in making a spiritual connection happen. God, or spirituality, is a song, a dance, an event, a celebration, that inspires a Red to action.

Reds love being around churches and religious activities. The heightened sense of expectancy, the electricity in the air, and the hustle and bustle all appeal to a Red. Celebration and the accompanying movement, dancing, singing, clapping, foot-stamping, and the joyous outpouring of emotions let a Red know that God, or spirituality, is not an abstract concept but humanity in motion. Reds are not transported by waves of rapture, as are Blues. They are engaged and available. Reds are here to be witnesses—to see with their own eyes, to hear with their own ears, to experience the validity of spiritual renewal and transformation. ''I am a new person'' would be the celebration song of a Red.

Once convinced, as a result of their own experience, Reds can become zealots because of their need to take action. Reds abhor a vacuum; they often rush headlong to fill it. If involved with a church or synagogue, they will move pews, string lights, set up sound systems, carry boxes of supplies, or walk miles proselytizing and distributing literature. They will do whatever is necessary to ensure the successful completion of a program or service because that is what they believe in. No task is too menial for a Red to do. Symbolically, this is the aura color that would wash the feet of Christ.

However, because Reds' physical sexual needs are at odds with the morality system of most organized mainstream religions, they often feel themselves to be unworthy. They have feelings of low self-esteem generated by their inability to live up to the lofty ideals of so many spiritual practices and systems. Reds know they are alive, loved, productive, creative, and valuable contributors when they can express themselves physically and sexually. They need ways to bridge the gap they perceive to exist between their needs and their beliefs. Religions often predict eternal separation from God if the rules regarding sex are not obeyed. This notion deprives Reds of the opportunity to be of service to humanity, at one with themselves, and at home with their own sense of the spiritual.

THE RED OVERLAY: ITS SPECIAL MEANING

Other colors augment themselves with overlays, but Reds seldom do. However, the Red as an overlay on other Personality Spectrums colors significantly alters the way in which that individual lives.

A Red overlay has extra attributes that make its meaning slightly different from that of Red as the primary personality aura color. A Red overlay is added to an aura as a conscious choice made between birth and three years of age in response to a situation in which a child finds himself or herself powerless as a consequence of adult behavior over which the child has no power or control. The Red overlay registers the abrupt, violent loss of physical safety and well-being without any compensating love and nurturing.

A Red overlay is added in one of three ways. First, it occurs if a child is born prematurely or has a physical problem at birth resulting in the use of radical medical procedures to sustain life. The overlay gets put into place, or comes to rest in the aura, because the child is too fragile or too sick for the normal parental bonding process to proceed. The Red overlay registers the terror, pain, and vulnerability the baby experienced, as if no amount of love will compensate for the loss of safety in the first moments of life.

Second, a child who has been physically or sexually abused as an infant—before three years of age—will put in a Red overlay, registering the loss of physical safety and corresponding lack of emotional compensation. Because this abuse takes place prior to the formation of language, at the preverbal stage of development, the child is unable to communicate its anguish and pain at the betrayal by the parent. This problem is different from that of a child who is sexually abused after the age of three and doesn't talk about it; this refusal does not come from the absence of language.

The third reason a Red overlay is added is emotional abandonment or betrayal. This can occur when the child is left to fend for itself in a situation inspiring terror or great emotional loss for which he or she has no emotional, physical, or spiritual resources, such as when a child is left to shift for itself after the birth of a sibling or the death or disappearance of a parent. The question the child asks is: Where are the adults in my life? Whom can I count on? Am I enough?

The outcome of having a Red overlay is the component of *rage*, the bottling of feelings of frustration and helplessness with no way of being able to get a handle on them. Reds with no overlay have the physical stamina to work out much of the backlog of energy that causes rage through hard, physical labor, or exercise. Other colors with the Red overlay do not necessarily have that access. Therefore, safe, productive outlets such as psychotherapy, bioenergetics, or gestalt therapy need to be found to release the emotional pressure that builds with the Red overlay. Boxing, pumping iron, or hard physical labor are all ways to vent the pressure so that the individual has access to the lusty side of himself or herself—the part of the self that loves life and is willing to let life love them.

FOUR

ORANGE

In the Personality Spectrums system, Orange is the color for individuals who need to test their own physical limitations against the environment. Fearless, powerful, heedless of their own personal safety, they shake their fists in the face of God.

The challenge for Oranges is to deal with our increasingly complex society. We are faced not so much with physical survival problems as with complicated moral and ethical questions. We are coping with the quality of life as opposed to simple survival.

An Orange prefers a challenge requiring physical courage. But our society forces us to tackle the frontier of the inner self, which requires spiritual courage. This question arises: Does an Orange have the ability to distinguish between these two kinds of courage—the courage required to face physical danger and risk as opposed to the courage required to come to terms with the inner self?

The lesson that is presented over and over again to an Orange is that there are physical limits and boundaries to human capabilities. Instead of constantly pushing to find out what those physical boundaries are, Oranges must learn to use that same energy to discover the inner dimensions of the self. The challenge for an Orange is to live long enough for age and experience to begin to allow the more obscure image of moral courage to come to the forefront of their consciousness.

APPROACH TO PHYSICAL REALITY

Oranges perceive themselves to be the cleverest, strongest, most cunning beasts in the animal kingdom. It is as if Oranges set out to prove that they are more cunning than a snake, more fleet than a deer, more agile than a monkey. Oranges seem to harness the mind to serve their bodies in a competition with the environment and all it contains.

Oranges love the thrill and excitement of physical challenge. The thought of bare-handed combat with a lion would keep most other Personality Spectrums colors awake at night in sheer terror, but Oranges relish the thought of such a challenge. An Orange would spend the night turning over the various scenarios. While other colors would be thinking over the potential for pain and injury, an Orange would contemplate how it would feel to be so alive, locked in a struggle for life. Unless the stakes are life and death, an Orange does not get a sense of satisfaction or thrill from accomplishment.

Oranges are the chameleons of the spectrum, taking on the mannerisms or the characteristics of their prey, their foe, or their physical environment. Whatever the challenge, Oranges register it as sensations within their physical body. Like Yellows, Oranges experience adrenaline rushes of excitement when they take on a challenge, whether it be climbing the rigging of a four-masted sailing vessel, dangling over the side of a sheer mountain wall, or tracking a wild animal. Oranges get a thrill from the danger they perceive themselves to be in.

Even as infants, Oranges accept the challenge of the physical environment. Furniture is seen as an obstacle to be conquered. Parents of toddlers who are Orange have their hands full keeping them off the tops of cabinets. But the Orange child is undaunted by the scrapes and bruises that result from climbing and exploring. The physical injuries cause more emotional pain for the parents than they do physical pain for Orange children. It is as if they have no memory of the pain; therefore, they can afford to take more risks. The challenge for parents is to learn how to give their children the freedom and space to develop the skills necessary to survive without becoming paranoid about their safety and longevity.

MENTAL ATTITUDES

Oranges tend to live in their heads, conceiving and planning the next challenge. However, Oranges cannot stay in the realm of imagination; they must see if they can actually *do* the imagined feat. They make elaborate preparations, mentally reviewing their strategy and plans before taking action. As they rehearse the scene in their minds, becoming comfortable with the various aspects of the event, they often peel away the safety devices that have been built into the plan, creating a greater risk to themselves and therefore a greater thrill when it occurs.

Oranges do not do well in our current educational system. Being stuck at a desk doing math problems causes them to feel resentment and anger that often look like indifference and boredom. They perceive the process of education as passive while they prefer to engage life actively. Because they do not fear pain, they are daredevils and often foolhardy. This behavior can cause them to create discipline problems in school and to alienate their peer group. They are very intelligent, but they are survivors rather than intellectuals who take pleasure in ideas and concepts.

Oranges use their education to plan a climb up Mount Everest, or to develop a stunt run for a movie scene. They are meticulous in their calculations, spending long hours mentally assessing the amount and number of supplies needed, gauging closely the balance between the chances of survival and the risk of death. They are *realists*. They prefer concrete reality to abstract theory.

Mentally, Oranges see everything in terms of physical advantages. They have the ability to view a situation from the perspective of their opponent—whether it is animate or inanimate. They pride themselves on being able to get inside the mind of their opponent, whether it is big game or the face of a mountain. It is as if they ask, "If I were that mountain, what would someone need in order to successfully climb me?" These thinking processes are part of the physical, emotional, and mental preparations that an Orange makes.

EMOTIONAL MAKEUP

Oranges vacillate between exhilaration and simply existing. For them, going to the grocery store, filling up the gas tank, and going on picnics are time fillers. For Oranges, to be faced with danger, a physical dare, or a life-threatening risk is to be alive, to be excited, to feel. Oranges know they are alive when they are standing in the crow's nest high above the heaving deck of a sailing ship, a challenge conquered.

Oranges are entirely self-centered in their relationship to life. The risks they take have only to do with their needs. Oranges are unable and unwilling to modify their behavior to accommodate the fears or concerns of loved ones. To risk their lives is to be *alive;* everything else is a form of *living death.* Therefore, Oranges cannot, and will not, play it safe for the sake of a mate or children.

Emotionally, Oranges are unavailable unless they are planning an event or retelling those they have lived through. Their emotional response is at the primitive level of human existence. This Personality Spectrums color does not seem to care for the nuances of human emotion, responding only to raw, physical courage and the passion that it arouses. Tenderness, compassion, and consideration for others have no real meaning for Oranges. They feel life as strong bold splashes of color, not weak pastels. Therefore, they do not form emotional bonds with others. Emotionally, they are loners, almost narcissistic in the emphasis they place on their needs and wants. This aura color seems to live out every man's fantasy of himself: to take the physical dare and to come home unscathed. Oranges also earn the respect, awe, and adulation of others, but they do not seem to care if the world is impressed by their feats. They do not do them for the benefit of others, only for themselves.

SOCIAL STYLE

To the Oranges, nothing matches the excitement of the challenge. Everything, including sex, takes second place. For them, sex is a release, a natural body function. Because most

Oranges are physically well built, fit, and trim, with a lepre-chaun's impish elusiveness, they are attractive to others and have no problem finding mates or partners. While sex is fun and pleasurable to them, it is not worth dying for. On the other hand, to hang off the side of Mount Everest at the top of the world—that is worth any risk.

COMPATIBILITY WITH OTHER COLORS

Physical (environmental) Colors

It is important to remember that Oranges tend to be the isolates of the Personality Spectrums. They are not team players; their only commitment is to themselves. Their very natures are opposed to the restraints of a relationship with another; they hate being accountable to a mate or children.

Reds and Oranges are not a good chemical mix. When they are together, the feeling is one of gears being stripped. Their issues are too much the same. There is too little padding between the rough spots of their personalities. Confrontations leave them angry and unfulfilled.

Oranges mating with Oranges is probably a fairly rare occurrence, given the volatile potential in this match. Since neither one wants to be dominated or controlled, there is essentially a standoff.

Magentas tend to set an Orange's teeth on edge. While they are both Physical (environmental) colors, the Orange measures success in terms of danger, and the Magenta measures success in skewing or warping aspects of reality. An Orange would find purple hair disgusting; a Magenta would think being a stunt driver childish.

Physical (body) Colors

Yellows are fascinated with the swashbuckling, swagger-ing bravado of Oranges of both sexes. However, the innocent Yellow is soon disenchanted with the pragmatic realism of an Orange's perspective. Yellows like to think that the danger and the daring is all a game, when for an Orange it is deadly serious.

Physical Tans and Oranges can create a truce for the purpose of living and being together as long as they both understand that this is a kind of marriage of convenience. Physical Tans can respond sexually to the demands and needs of an Orange while at the same time giving them the physical and emotional space they seem to require. Oranges seem to understand the natural reticence of the Physical Tan and do not push for more communication than the Physical Tan can give.

Mental Colors

Mental Tans appreciate the meticulous care with which Oranges plan and prepare for the exciting challenges. What they don't understand is the utter lack of concern for physical safety and security. To a Mental Tan, living on the edge the way Oranges do is taking unnecessary risks with a high probability of failure. This does not make good sense to Mental Tans and, to the detriment of the relationship, they will say so over and over and over. Oranges find this obsession with safety boring.

Oranges are attracted to Greens the way moths are attracted to candle flame. The bright sparkle of a Green's mind, combined with the capacity to lay out strategy and plan the logistics of challenges, entrances an Orange. If an Orange were ever to consider settling down, it would be with a Green because a Green vicariously lives the thrills with the Orange without making the Orange feel guilty.

Nurturing Tans are not attracted to the high-profile personality of the Orange. Nurturing Tans fail to see how excitement, drama, and daredevilry serve to enhance the quality of life.

It is nearly impossible for Loving Tans and Oranges to communicate with one another. The Loving Tans are trying to figure everything out in their heads while the Oranges are sorting equipment and gear on the floor. Loving Tans stand by helplessly while the Oranges pack everything up.

Emotional/Spiritual Colors

The Emotional/Spiritual personality colors are the antithesis of the Orange's physical process. Their communication styles are like two ships passing in the night; they do not seem to see or hear each other. With Violets, the danger for Oranges is that they can get into power struggles that can lead to some very rigid battle lines being drawn between the two colors.

PERSONAL POWER AND LEADERSHIP STYLE

Oranges are a spectator sport all by themselves. Evel Knievel's jump across the Snake River on a motorcycle was a challenge, a feat that horrified and fascinated many people. In other words, Oranges are not leaders, per se; they stand out from the crowd because they are respected and held in awe. They are willing to go off and do their own thing, asking no one for permission, expecting nothing in return, not even adulation. When others perceive them as heroes, no one is more surprised than an Orange. For an Orange, heroes are those people who do something well when, if given a choice, they would not do it at all. Because Oranges *enjoy* climbing around on steel I-beams thirty stories above the ground, they do not consider that act heroic. On the other hand, for an Orange to live quietly in the suburbs would constitute a heroic action.

Oranges leave leadership to others—the ship's captain, the expedition's leader, the film director. They have no interest in or talent for administrative aspects of a project. They simply want to be free to do their own thing—to set up the stunt scene, do the dry run, light the fires, ignite the gas tanks, and wreck the cars while the film rolls. Oranges prefer to operate autonomously; however, they will join a group so that others will solve the everyday problems, relieving them of that burden so they can spend more energy on physical feats.

As competitors, Oranges choose individual rather than team sports. They like high-speed auto racing, for example, because it allows them to test their physical prowess, mental agility, and courage. Their first challenge is the automobile: Will it do what it is designed to do? The second is the environment—the weather, track, distance, and time. Only then are they concerned with the competition between themselves and other drivers.

FINANCIAL CHOICES

When our country was new and wild, Oranges had little trouble providing the necessities of life. When they were hungry, they simply went out into the forest and trapped an animal for food. As civilization has encroached, Oranges have taken a passive approach to the issue of money and finances. They are neither entrepreneurs nor employers. They tend to free-lance, maintaining their personal freedom. They only want to be paid for what they do best—provide thrills and take risks. They do well when they are sponsored by companies who gain publicity from their efforts.

The needs of an Orange are few and simple, but they are not inexpensive. In whatever arena Oranges choose to take their risks, the tools they use must be the finest money can buy. Mountain climbing gear will be of the highest quality; snorkeling equipment will be the best on the market. While other Personality Spectrums colors may choose this same equipment based on brand name, price, or discount percentage, Oranges are interested only in quality.

Money has no meaning for an Orange. If something is not a question of life or death, an Orange considers it nonessential. Because Oranges live on the jagged edge, risking death frequently, they have little appreciation for long-range financial planning. Intuitively, Oranges know that they will have a relatively short life span. In their typically shortsighted fashion, they neglect to plan for their mates and children. To confront that responsibility would be to have to come to terms with the major issue of their life—to differentiate between physical and moral courage. The trick for Oranges is to convert their physical courage into moral courage, choosing issues as challenges rather than ill-considered physical risks.

CAREER OPTIONS

Oranges are the daredevils of society, choosing careers in which physical danger and courage combine with a devil-may-care attitude toward personal safety. They prefer occupations that allow them to ride the jagged edge of life. Oranges may work as steeplejacks, frogmen, bomb squad members, explorers, or stunt men and women. They choose situations based on their need to test their own physical prowess against the environment. They see all of life as a contest, a duel to the death.

SPIRITUALITY

Oranges have no wish to be confined within the physical confines of a church building or by the moral and intellectual strictures of an ideology or philosophy. Their search for spirituality is really a search for a meaning in life beyond themselves. When they have climbed the world's highest peak or plumbed the depths of the Atlantic Rift, what else is there for them to explore? Outer space is dominated by technicians and engineers. The only frontier left to an Orange is the inner self.

Until they are willing to confront their inner selves, Oranges constantly seem to be throwing themselves at the head of God in a dare that only they and God know about. Those with this aura color seem awesome to others. However, a true test of courage for Oranges would be to confront themselves, to go into the void that is within. They often choose to embark on spectacular feats in an effort to avoid those who would ask them to evaluate the difference between moral courage and physical courage. To come face to face with truth, acknowledging one's limitations while at the same time being willing to move forward, is a true act of courage. It is the fortitude that allows us to create quality lives full of promise and meaning. For an Orange, this is the final act of courage. This is the ultimate risk.

FIVE

MAGENTA

The key to understanding the Magenta Personality Spectrums color is their unwillingness to conform to the expectations and norms set by society. These individuals seek to express their individuality by using, with creativity and flair, the belongings and raw materials at their disposal. Because they look at life through a magenta filter, they tend to be viewed as the nonconformists of the spectrum.

The single most difficult thing for a Magenta is to understand the difference between commitment and entrapment. For a Magenta to be locked into a nine-to-five job, to be married and have children, and to run a household would be a form of insanity. They need to learn to create for themselves a life-style that works for them and does not impinge on the sensibilities of others. Magentas revitalize our concept of creativity by offering a new perspective, opening new vistas, and exploring new points of departure.

APPROACH TO PHYSICAL REALITY

Reds want to subdue reality, and Oranges want to conquer it; Magentas want to push physical reality to the leaky margins—that locale where fantasy and reality become a blur. Magentas consider life worth living only if they can listen to their own inner drummer. They live on the edge, creating a three-dimensional physical environment in their mind's eye

63

that is very different from the one we experience in our day-to-day existence.

Magentas create in the physical environment in ways that are similar to those of their sister Personality Spectrums colors, Red and Orange. They prefer products to abstractions. Magentas work with the tangible but creative material aspects of the world. They find their greatest satisfaction when manipulating, working with, changing, or building something real and specific. So much the better if it is outrageous, off-the-wall, and controversial.

Their innovative, creative, fertile minds lead them to explore the unusual, bizarre, arty, or trendy. Their nonconformity allows them to skew their perspective on the world, making them unique. Out of this new, fresh perspective comes the gift of this color—creating experiences that allow the rest of us to see the world from an alternative point of view. It is as if the Magentas ask us to put on three-D glasses, turning our flat two-dimensional world into one with depth and perspective. Everyday life looks quite different.

Magentas are outrageous, and they prefer it that way. They take pride in their refusal to adapt to any of society's mechanisms of lock step thinking or behavior. By creating a totally original point of view, Magentas give us an opportunity to laugh at ourselves. They encourage us to find ways to express our own divergent individuality by expressing their own.

MENTAL ATTITUDES

Magentas have bright, agile minds—fleet as quicksilver. However, they are unwilling to master acres of boring details. They become experts in the field that interests them, or in which they might choose to make a living. But if they do not see much need for information, they refuse to clutter their minds with inessential details. Like the other Physical (environmental) colors, the Magentas are strong-willed and determined about the things they regard as important. They are eclectic in their learning. They can be excellent students when the subject interests them or they see a need to learn about it.

Otherwise a Magenta will move heaven and earth to create a diversion—preferably one that entertains the entire class. School subjects that appeal to inquiring minds, taught by teachers who are flexible and creative, are ideally suited to a Magenta. Magentas do well in drama, English, debate, forensics, the arts, science (if allowed to "play" in the labs), physical education, and crafts such as woodworking and welding.

Magentas need to develop the ability to stay with a project until it is completed. Each new project is like a silver lure, sparkling and twisting through the water, distracting the attention of the Magentas from what they are supposed to be doing. Learning to finish a job is one of the most difficult challenges for a Magenta. Short projects that are easy to bring to conclusion build confidence and pride in the Magenta. Once the Magenta experiences the satisfaction of accomplishment, it becomes easier for him or her to stay focused for longer and longer periods of time. This is one of the major skills necessary to the Magentas' happiness and well-being—it allows them a wider range of career choices and a greater chance of success.

Their mental process appears to be haphazard when, in fact, most Magentas have a very clear idea of what they want to create, say, or do. Because their nature is to stretch the limits of everything they encounter—products, social customs, mores, relationships, and standards by which most of us judge and evaluate our reality—Magentas are constantly searching for new and different ways to use everyday items. Many Magentas are inventors of those handy gadgets that the rest of us couldn't get along without. They are continually fascinated by what is in the marketplace.

EMOTIONAL MAKEUP

The greatest problem for Magentas is loneliness. Few people can tolerate the skewed perspective so natural for a Magenta. When they attempt to conform, Magentas lose touch with what makes life worth living for them, and this often plunges them into deep despair. Female Magentas are often programmed by society to believe that the fastest road to happiness lies in being like a Blue—the natural caretaker of the spectrum. However, for Magenta women this is the fastest road to madness.

Magentas are basically loners. They don't mean to be and they are not always pleased that they have difficulty finding compatible mates and partners. However, their work habits, living arrangements, and restless energy make it difficult for them to create and foster long-term loving relationships. Their lives are often filled with happy chances or disastrous snafus and miscommunications. They neither want nor need to be organized, and this trait keeps some potential mates away. A Magenta needs to ask this question when beginning a relationship: How much confusion and disorganization is too much? Until a Magenta can answer that question, a relationship will last only as long as the other individual's ability to tolerate ambiguity.

Their quicksilver vibrancy, eclectic ideas, and outrageous solutions to simple problems make Magentas attractive and fun to be with. However, living all of life on the brink can be tiring for most of the other Personality Spectrums colors. When one is courting, coleslaw for dinner at 3:00 A.M. is the stuff of memories. But for a Magenta, that's *life*. The question they ask is: Doesn't everyone eat dinner at 3:00 A.M.?

Emotionally, Magentas are reacting to the confinement of their parents' expectations: get good grades, clean your room, make a few good friends, and participate in school, church, or neighborhood activities. To the Magenta, these requirements seem like life sentences, as crippling to their personality as the Chinese foot-binding custom would be to their feet. These children need to explore their environment and interact dynamically with it. These are the children who want to try something just because it is there. Magentas may conform temporarily in order to please their parents. When they go out on their own, however, they will explore the limits of their tangible reality.

One of the first things they do is to choose extreme styles in hairdos and clothing. But their extremes are zany rather than ugly or bizarre. They love authentic innovation, and are especially good at showing fads for what they are—mindless.

Magentas will take various fad garments and combine them in such a way as to make a new statement. Their fashion sense is one of fun, not anger.

Magentas can swing between high and low moods. The highs are expressions of freedom, sense of self, acceptance, and creativity. The lows result from trying to please others, loss of sense of self, and finding no way out of a mundane or humdrum existence. They can lessen the severity of these mood swings by choosing careers or occupations that allow or even encourage them to develop their own style. Artistic pursuits—sign painting, staging of rock bands, performing as a mime or a clown—offer opportunities to build a bridge between the inner reality of the self and the outer reality of society. They can also choose to live in those parts of the country or world where they are less conspicuous in their uniqueness. A Magenta in a small town will have more difficulty than a Magenta in San Francisco or New York City.

SOCIAL STYLE

Magentas love people. They are the madcaps of the spectrum—full of fun, willing to be outrageous, daring to do the things the rest of us wish we had the courage to do. They entertain with laughter, fun, skits, and foolishness. When you are invited to a Magenta's home, you never know what you will be in for. When they allow their imaginations free rein, a luau on the fire escape of a New York walk-up would not be an impossibility.

The only way to enjoy a Magenta's party, social life, or friendship is to get into the swing of things. Magentas are unpredictable, nonconforming, and relatively oblivious to rigid social customs. Magentas are without malice; they are not angry, nor are they antisocial. They simply have a different view of life. Often, when the pressure to conform becomes too great, they create their own hilarious backlash. Even when confronted with painful, restrictive childhoods, Magentas intuitively know that laughter is the best medicine. They enjoy the absurdities of life. Only a Magenta would have a pink plastic flamingo as a living room centerpiece.

Magentas find unusual things to see and do wherever they are. The more outrageous the event or activity, the more fun. They love mixing up their realities. When Magentas need a lift, they invite all their friends to attend a silent film and make up a story to go along with the action on the screen.

Magentas make friends wherever they go. Every encounter is an opportunity for them to get to know how others think and feel. Magentas collect a wide spectrum of friends who are as eclectic as their agglomeration of home decorating items. They take comfort in listening to the ways other people break away from their own bonds of conformity. The unifying factor among the friendships and relationships formed by a Magenta is that there is no unifying factor. They collect people with unusual occupations and interests the way some of us collect stamps, appreciating them for their beauty, their art, and their individuality.

Because most of their friends are as footloose as they are, they do not establish the tight bonds of caretaking that are often taken for granted by other Personality Spectrums colors. That is not to say that Magentas are not considerate or caring. They prefer to be relieved from the pressure (and fear) of confining or stultifying responsibility of caring for another person. Occasionally their feelings get hurt when they think they have been ignored, but hurt feelings are a small price to pay in exchange for being relieved of the burden of responsibility.

Magentas tend to marry often, not out of fickleness or an inability to maintain long-term relationships, but because they feel that when they have learned all the life lessons they can from a given relationship, it is time to move on. They also marry because they know that commitment enhances a couple's opportunity to learn from the experience of being together. Magentas also love to be the guest of honor at a party—and what more appropriate party than their own wedding?

Magentas also have a facility for departing from relationships in such a way as to leave the other person emotionally, physically, and spiritually intact. Magentas are not destroyers. They are learners and experimenters; they are the participant-observer within a culture of their own creation. They remain friends with their former mates, often regarding them as part of an extended family, so to speak.

Individuals who marry frequently or who have had many serial relationships are not necessarily Magentas. Magentas are distinctive in that they choose their partners carefully for the life lessons a relationship with them offers. In addition, the Magenta's partners are usually aware that the relationship, even though they have gone through a marriage ceremony, is not necessarily permanent.

COMPATIBILITY WITH OTHER COLORS

Physical (environmental) Colors

Reds tend to be too solid and steady to pique the interest of a Magenta for long. Also, when Reds get their feelings hurt, they tend to clam up. This silent treatment drives the Magentas wild, and they are likely to find someone else to amuse them. By the time the Reds come around, the Magentas will be gone—physically and emotionally.

Oranges take themselves too seriously to appeal to Magentas. Magentas may be fascinated, however, by the Oranges' independence—the feeling that they do not need anyone, including the Magentas. This frees the Magentas from the fear that the relationship will overwhelm and smother them.

A Magenta mated to a Magenta would be difficult because there would never be anybody at home—literally or figuratively. Because they both have such a laissez-faire attitude toward the details of life, checking accounts would be in a shambles, and the refrigerator would be full of things growing their own penicillin.

Physical (body) Colors

Yellow mated to Magenta is like a marriage of two best friends and childhood playmates who are now grown up. Magentas are strong enough and mature enough to do all the fun things that most Yellows only fantasize about. The relationship between a Yellow and a Magenta would be based on experiencing the joy in life. However, neither Personality Spectrums color is adept at handling the crises of life.

Physical Tans are too quiet and introspective to appeal to a Magenta for long. Magentas' conversations are a stream of consciousness. Physical Tans do not want all that information, nor do they know what to do with it. So they do nothing. Therefore, the Magenta can be shut out of the Physical Tan's life.

Mental Colors

Mental Tans are too staid and proper for the shenanigans and high jinks that appeal to a Magenta. However, the Mental Tans can give the Magentas a sense of safety and security in which to explore their own artistic, creative expression. In exchange, the Mental Tans require appreciation and intellectual rapport.

Greens see the potential inherent within the Magenta's way of life and the possibilities of successful financial ventures. The Magenta and Green are well matched intellectually because the Green can leap to wherever the Magenta's fertile imagination wanders. The Magenta needs an outcome or product, and the Green sees the marvelous potentialities of each idea. The intellectual camaraderie between these two colors can lead to high emotional and sexual fulfillment for both.

Nurturing Tans are amused by the machinations of the Magenta. However, the need for security and the desire to work within the system make most Nurturing Tans unwilling to live on the creative edge with a Magenta.

Loving Tans and Magentas both tend to take relationships lightly; the partner or mate is not the focus of their life. Therefore, the relationship between a Magenta and a Loving Tan could easily turn platonic because neither of these colors is willing to be the strong emotional generating force within the relationship.

Emotional/Spiritual Colors

Blues and Magentas seem to speak different languages. The Blue wants to get married and settle down, and the Magenta wants to go to New York City. The Blue wants emotional security, and the Magenta wants an open marriage. The Blue wants to know what went wrong, and the Magenta wants out. The Physical (environmental) attributes of the Magenta run counter to the needs of the Emotional/Spiritual Blue.

Violets and Magentas seem to spark off each other emotionally and physically, generating and reinforcing the creative force within each of them. Violets imagine and describe the new product for which they see a need, and a Magenta can produce a prototype out of the stuff in a junk drawer in the kitchen. This Magenta ability to come up with solutions is an emotional and spiritual turn-on for the Violet. If the Violet can stay flexible, this match can be dynamic and fun.

Lavenders think like Magentas, but they do so in the realm of fantasy and dreams, whereas Magentas dwell in three-dimensional reality. These two colors have many emotional and mental characteristics in common; however, their similarities also tend to be the bones of contention within a relationship. The main difficulty is similar to that of Magentas mated together: Who is minding the store?

Crystals and Magentas are like fire and water. Crystals are silent and deep, requiring long periods of quiet, isolation, and prayerful retreat. Magentas must be going and doing every minute, filling their lives with excitement and productivity. A Crystal wants a home that is a sanctuary; a Magenta wants a home that is a layover stop. These two colors would have to negotiate everything within the relationship, and a Magenta is not interested in working that hard.

Indigos are amused by Magentas but generally not enamored of them. The Magentas' hectic pace in life, exuberance, and enthusiasm have no place in the scheme of things for an Indigo. Both colors have the ability to see life from an altered perspective, but they may not see it from the same one.

PERSONAL POWER AND LEADERSHIP STYLE

The Magentas' personal power lies in their willingness to set their own rules no matter the ramifications, since conforming to social norms and expectations is so physically painful for them. Their solution is to move to places, usually large cities, where their uniqueness can be absorbed in the milieu and where they can blend into the cityscape. They choose friends who appreciate their alternative view of life, and they avoid people who insist on doing things the way they have always been done. Magentas don't care how things have always been done. In fact, that is no recommendation at all to the Magentas. Their response is "Why?" For them, change is the essence of being; change allows them to feel safe and in control of their environment. Whereas most colors need a sense of familiarity in their lives, to Magentas sameness is death, not safety.

Magentas are not leaders in the accepted sense of the word. They are not organized, nor do they have the dynamic personal power and charisma we associate with good leaders. Instead, Magentas lead by showing us the stagnation in our lives. By painting larger-than-life cans of tomato soup, Andy Warhol asked us to reconsider what we regard as important. Magentas lead by understanding what they experience on the inner planes of their psyches. They then have the courage to act on that information, making portions of their environment conform to their view of their inner space. Magentas are not rebellious, nor is their creative expression especially angry. They simply see reality differently than most people do, and they attempt to somehow bring their environment into harmony and balance with their internal perspective.

FINANCIAL CHOICES

Magentas are members of the Physical (environmental) Family; therefore, they always seem to have a handle on how the world of physical reality operates. They know what they have to do to make money, spend it creatively, and still meet their financial obligations.

Most important, they are able to play with money. Food and shelter are the necessary stage props. But in all else, Magentas need and want to be creative. To a Magenta, those products and ideas that are creative, thought-provoking, or imaginative are the true necessities of life. Magentas are apt to think that a trip to the neighborhood thrift shop is more important than buying salad makings—unless, of course, they are planning a Mexican fiesta and need lettuce for tacos.

Money for a Magenta is the ticket to new experiences, new ideas, and new ways of doing things. Magentas love to travel, to explore other countries, to mix with the people and live among them. They can be seen folk dancing in the town square and learning to speak the local language from children. Magentas are the free spirits of the spectrum and travel with the protection provided charmed individuals.

Magentas can also be practical and down to earth about money. They know the value of a dollar; they just don't want to be tied down by that value system. In their finances, as in all other aspects of their lives, Magentas know the value and meaning of living each moment as it comes. They are not much interested in deferred gratification, but they have a healthy respect for the here and now.

CAREER OPTIONS

Magentas do well in occupations that have a great deal of flexibility, creativity, and potential for innovative ideas and inventions. They need jobs and careers that require little supervision (such as art therapy with disturbed children) or, conversely, a great deal of supervision (such as acting under a strong director).

The ideal careers for Magentas are those wherein they can make a great deal of money during a short period of concentrated effort. This gives them the financial flexibility to take time off to explore different aspects of themselves and their environment. Any career in the performing arts would serve them nicely. They do especially well in all forms of comedy—improvisational, stand-up, and comic acting.

Because they are so ingenious, they can work independently as artists, inventors, or writers. They can take advantage of short, intense periods of creative, fertile solitude. They do not necessarily need the inspiration or motivation that comes from being with others. However, they do need a representative or agent to supervise their work from drawing board to production. They are not interested in the details, but are strongly aware of bottom lines and financial outcomes.

Magentas do well in any career or occupation on the leading edge. Such jobs appeal to their fascination with the bright, the young, and the new. For example, they would be good as art directors, photographers, or designers for slick new magazines. The Magenta would love to investigate, photograph, or sell whatever product or idea is the latest and hottest in clothes, music, people, entertainment, and travel.

Magentas make excellent salespeople, especially when they are selling toys—makeup, clothes, antiques, or concepts. They entice the customer into the fantasy and *then* make the sales pitch. Because of this ability to live in their fantasy, Magentas also make good entrepreneurs. They are capable of dynamically visualizing success, and then making the imagined goal a reality.

SPIRITUALITY

As the nonconformists of the spectrum, Magentas are unwilling to be bound by any convention, set of rules, or code of laws regulating behavior, attitudes, or beliefs. Magentas will only stay involved with a system or organization as long as they are free to come and go as they please, taking what they need and returning when they need replenishment or renewal.

Magentas, as one of the Physical (environmental) Personality Spectrums colors, have a strong connection to the earth. Religious practices that are too mental or emotional do not appeal to Magentas. They need to be grounded in their spirituality; they prefer outdoor services or activities that put them in direct communion with nature.

Magentas have a close connection with nature because plants and animals make no demands on them other than that they be allowed to coexist. Magentas find solace in nature, an acceptance of who they are at the core. Walks in the woods or the park and planting, tending, or harvesting crops are ways in which Magentas express their spirituality. Any retreat facility would do well to have a Magenta on staff—to tend to the ecology and to educate guests and participants in the relationship between nature, humanity, and spirituality.

Magentas are reluctant to join any church or organization. They are unwilling to commit themselves for fear of being tied down. They resent demands being made on them that they cannot be sure of fulfilling. Like the other Physical (environment) colors, Magentas can be depended upon once they give their word—but they do not often give their word. They prefer to keep all their options open, to be able to come and go within a group or an organization as they feel the need to learn and grow. They prefer loosely knit organizations to those that are more rigidly structured because they like to feel that the door is open for them.

For Magentas, religious services and rituals need to be more practical and utilitarian than those offered by most religions. For all their zaniness, Magentas can be very down-to-earth. They see the value in the cycle of the seasons, with the attendant duties and responsibilities within each season. Through the enactment of ritual, they can attune their lives to the seasons. By being able to concentrate on metaphysical as well as physical concerns, Magentas can maintain balance and emotional stability in their lives. This sense of balance in turn gives them a centeredness, a sense of who they are and what their purpose in life is.

SIX

YELLOW

Yellows are those people most affected by the body's sensitive biochemical balance. When they are not careful, they are susceptible to physical addiction—bodily cravings. Yellows need to learn to recognize and act on the signals their bodies send them.

The best way for Yellows to measure their own success is by the amount of joy they are experiencing in life. It is when they experience joy that Yellows come to know God. To experience joy is to be congruent with one's inner being and to express it appropriately at work and play. Of all the colors, it is the Yellows' obligation to organize their lives so that everything they do gives them personal satisfaction. It is by this example that they teach.

APPROACH TO PHYSICAL REALITY

Yellows make sense out of the world through the biochemical sensations they experience in their bodies. They are one of the kinesthetic Personality Spectrums colors; this means that they have a physical reaction to a situation *before* they have either an emotional or intellectual response. When Yellows walk into a room full of people, they know immediately if they want to stay. Their bodies register and evaluate the kind of energy in the room, telling them whether to remain. Yellows have acute biological mechanisms that respond to situations, places, events, and people. Unlike Physical Tans, who sense through their reflex muscle action, Yellows sense the nuances of life through their biochemistry. This makes Yellows very impressionable to nonverbal communication, which they register but have difficulty explaining to themselves or to others. Yellows who feel trapped in a meeting or at a party will exhibit twitchy or restless behaviors such as foot-tapping or table-drumming. They do not mean to be rude; their body is telling them to keep moving. The challenge for others is to help Yellows recognize this information and to choose appropriate ways to act on it.

Because of the overstimulation of the biochemical system throughout the day and the lack of stimulation when they are asleep at night, Yellows often greet the morning with a sense of low-level pain, achiness, or uneasiness. They are not sure just where the pain is because they do not know how to translate it into information that will assist them in making sense out of the world. They often attempt to camouflage the pain by substituting a pleasant sensation that they can accept and relate to. The easiest way for them to mask the pain, especially in the morning, is by taking an analgesic: coffee, white sugar, drugs, alcohol, or tobacco. Many Yellows start their day with four or five cups of coffee, a cola drink, or sweets . . . or some of everything.

The day can be a series of pain crises which a Yellow can handle in a positive or negative way. Yellows can become physically dependent on chemical substances for their sense of well-being, ingesting various stimulants throughout the day.

Other colors experience psychological addiction. For them, however, when the emotional issue is dealt with, so is the addiction. For Yellows this is not true. Since they process the world through their physical bodies, they do not always understand the enormous number of physical stimuli they experience.

The goal for Yellows is to find positive ways to handle or manage their physical pain or dis-ease. The trick is to fool their bodies by becoming addicted to other biochemicals that are naturally produced within the body and that are not harmful. It has been shown, for example, that during certain kinds of physical exercise, the brain releases endorphins. Several peptides secreted in the brain have a pain-relieving effect like that of morphine and give a heightened sense of well-being. For Yellows, it is better to be addicted to their own endorphins than to potentially dangerous substances.

For Yellows life is a balancing scale. On one side are the negatively addicting substances:

- Caffeine: Coffee, colas, chocolate
- Processed foods: White sugar, white flour
- Drugs: Over-the-counter, prescription, and illegal drugs, tobacco, marijuana
- Alcohol: Wine, beer, hard liquor

On the positive side of the scale are the natural endorphins produced in the body, which give Yellows a sense of peace. Several activities can help a Yellow produce these substances:

- Sex
- Exercise
- Prayer and meditation

Yellows need an active sex life for two reasons: because sexual activity is a form of physical exercise and because sexual release carries with it a sense of well-being that Yellows can get in no other way. At the moment of orgasm, a Yellow can reach out, touch the higher self, and know the joy that accompanies bliss. Sexual activity releases a biochemical surge of well-being, of feeling safe and at home in the world. This feeling may last for an entire day. At these times, Yellows wake up in the morning with stars in their eyes. When they feel safe and contented, Yellows are able to concentrate on developing skills and talents that will enhance their self-esteem and self-respect.

Physical exercise must be a part of every Yellow's day. Jogging, walking, swimming, bicycling, tennis, dancing, and other long-muscle activities that work the long muscles consistently are recommended. Forty-five minutes of this activity each day will allow the flood of biochemicals to flow through the system. Yellows should avoid activities such as high-impact aerobics, which pound or jam your skeletal structure and minimize the beneficial effect of the exercise regimen by causing stress to the joints and vertebrae. Yellows are very susceptible to knee, elbow, shoulder, and back injuries.

T'ai Chi, aikido, and Yoga are active forms of prayer and meditation which, for a Yellow, represent a third kind of positive addiction. Active forms of meditation are those that focus the mind on the body. Such meditation helps fill a Yellow's need for natural endorphins. In addition, it allows them to alter their state of awareness naturally, rather than artificially. As the mind becomes focused, the body becomes quiet, allowing inspiration, new ideas, and solutions to flood in. Not only are the Yellows tuning the body, they are also tuning the soul.

MENTAL ATTITUDES

Yellows are bright and creative. Since their bodies will not let them sit still long enough to gather data, they are not intellectuals. Their mental skills are in the realm of practical application; they can be most brilliant when applying what they learn in a practical way.

Yellows love learning when it is combined with the kinesthetic processes; they are happy and feel good about themselves. Because they are a kinesthetic color, they learn by doing; a hands-on approach works well for them. For example, because Yellows cannot sit still for extended periods of time, they need learning situations that allow them to process and absorb what they have learned through physical activity. If Yellows are required to sit too long, they will not retain information after a certain point. Instead they will attend to a body that has signaled data overload. This Personality Spectrums color learns well by listening to facts on a mini–tape recorder while jogging. Engaging the body in any learning process cements the knowledge for this aura color. Teachers, supervisors, and trainers of Yellows need to use hands-on methods and offer plenty of stretch breaks to allow for integration of the information.

EMOTIONAL MAKEUP

Yellows are like puppies—lovable, eager to please, affectionate, full of fun, loyal, and trustworthy. Yellows' natural openness makes it difficult for them to conceal anything. They are naive; their feelings are easily hurt and never hidden.

Yellows hate to see anyone angry, hurt, or in pain. They handle their discomfort in these situations by distracting themselves and others, substituting another activity instead of trying to solve the problem at hand. Yellows often tell jokes or make wisecracks at inappropriate moments because of their need to avoid confrontation. When a tangle of conflicting feelings and needs arises, a Yellow will ignore the situation and pretend it doesn't exist.

Yellows seem to be more childlike, as opposed to childish, than other colors. They are more open, filled with awe and wonder at the world around them. Yellows exhibit an innocence and trust that is refreshing. They are eager to explore and experience the world much the way children experience Disneyland for the first time—running to and fro exuberantly. Cynicism has no place in a Yellow, and therefore they often appear too trusting for their own good. This is not an act; it is the Yellows' natural way of being in the world. As they connect with the child within themselves, they express a love of life. When interacting with people who love and appreciate their talents, Yellows are at peace with themselves and know God through the joy they feel and express.

SOCIAL STYLE

Friendly, active, open, full of fun, Yellows love to have a good time. They love people and the outdoors. Activities such as picnics, baseball games, and days at the beach are ideally suited to them.

This Personality Spectrums color is the spontaneous party planner. Every club or organization needs one to serve as hospitality or social chairperson, for Yellows always seem to be the ones to organize the company picnic and the neighborhood baseball game. Because they are so eager to play, they assume everyone else is, too. By the time sides have been chosen and the first awkwardness has worn off, others have joined in the spirit of the game, thanks to the energetic insistence of the Yellow. They play for fun, exhibiting great patience with others. They truly understand that it is the group that is important in team sports; they play to enjoy the camaraderie, the shared experience.

To outsiders, Yellows seem to be always on the go, having a good time, surrounded by friends and companions. Yellows also have a quiet side to them. This is the part of them that needs family, home, security, a sense of belonging. Because of their trusting and open nature, Yellows often find themselves taken advantage of. A mate or family is their bulwark against the world—a safe harbor when things go wrong.

Because Yellows have a high sex drive, they often marry young. An early marriage can be dangerous to Yellows, however. They may get stuck in the adolescent perception of the mate as the source of gratification for all their needs, and as a result, they may fail to develop the adult skills of partnership and parenting. On the other hand, if they find someone who is able to nurture them and help them grow into new levels of their abilities and skills, they can truly find happiness and fulfillment within the marital relationship.

COMPATIBILITY WITH OTHER COLORS

Physical (environmental) Colors

Reds seem to anchor Yellows, giving them a sense of security and permanence. They both are willing to work; therefore, they are seldom without money. However, they are not much interested in long-range planning. Therefore, they can get into the habit of living on the edge.

Oranges are too intense, too self-conscious, and too focused on their own needs to be effective mates for Yellows. Yellows need and want a shared relationship, and Oranges do not.

Magentas and Yellows both have a playful outlook on life; however, the Magentas are more sophisticated and calculating.

A Yellow tumbles along through life, whereas the Magenta tends to have a goal, no matter how obtuse or inconvenient the destination. What they primarily share is a marvelous sense of humor.

Physical (body) Colors

Yellows mated to Yellows are playmates. They are a joy to behold. The problem is similar to that of Magentas mated to Magentas: Who will mind the store? Yellows are the ingenues, the ones easily taken advantage of. A mate of the same color provides no ballast against the storms of life.

Physical Tans and Yellows have a great deal in common. However, the Physical Tan tends to be too reticent for the Yellow, who needs someone to talk to. The Yellow tends to demand time and attention the Physical Tan is reluctant to give.

Mental Colors

Mental Tans provide the intellectual component, and the Yellows provide the personality. Mental Tans provide the logical, step-by-step planning skills; the Yellow can carry out the assignments. Whether in a marriage or a construction company, these two colors make ideal partners.

Yellows do not provide Greens with the mental stimulation that they find so attractive in many of the other colors. Therefore, these two colors have fewer areas of compatibility to draw on. The Green is not one to wait around while the Yellow is figuring something out, and the Yellow hates to get left behind. Therefore, some areas of serious disagreement can open up between these two colors.

Nurturing Tans provide emotional ballast for Yellows by listening to them with the heart instead of with the head. Yellows are so eager to please, so anxious to help others, that they often overextend themselves and their resources. A Nurturing Tan is able to provide the emotional support so necessary to a Yellow.

The Loving Tan is too abstract for the Yellow, who is

firmly rooted in physical reality. A Loving Tan who is waxing eloquent on some theory or another will totally lose the interest of a Yellow. Yellows try to listen politely, but they eventually lose interest and leave.

Emotional/Spiritual Colors

Blues and Yellows are ideal pairs. They both love helping people. Blues love to listen and to help out with emotional problems; Yellows love to help with physical problems such as planting the garden. Both these colors believe in "happily ever after" and are reluctant to take off their rose-colored glasses.

Violets and Yellows are the antithesis of one another. Yellows are eager and helpful; they see the best in everyone and everything. Violets tend to be cynical; they are the curmudgeons of the spectrum. They are more realistic about the motives of people. With a Violet, Yellows always feel that they have to defend everything they say and do. This does not make for a good balance in a relationship.

Lavenders and Yellows can have a very satisfactory sexual relationship, because the Lavenders feel safe in revealing their most secret fantasies to Yellows. However, because these two colors are so different in other ways, they have little in common out of the bedroom. Lavenders want to drift and dream and Yellows want to be involved with people.

Crystals find the exuberance of the Yellow difficult to bear. Crystals prefer a reclusive, quiet life-style, and Yellows love being the life of the party. Crystals become agitated when they are around a crowd of people too long; a Yellow thrives as the center of attention.

Indigos are willing to sit back and observe life, whereas Yellows need to get in and participate. Yellows tend to take on more than they can handle, and when they look to the Indigo to assist them, the Indigo is emotionally and physically unavailable. It is as if the Indigo is saying, "You got yourself into this. Now you get yourself out." Yellows are at first confused by this apparently cold behavior, then angered by it. They feel abandoned and unsupported.

PERSONAL POWER AND LEADERSHIP STYLE

Yellow is one of the three *leadership* colors, the other two being Mental Tan and Violet. Yellows lead out of sheer joy in being with people. Their infectious laughter, good sense of humor, and easygoing attitude make them well-liked, but not feared or held in awe. They do not have the strength to wage interoffice warfare, nor are they ruthless enough to climb their way to the top of the corporate ladder. Instead, they inspire confidence by their eagerness to help, their willingness to share their time and talent, and their patience and good humor.

Yellows lead by *doing*. They love to demonstrate their skill or craft. Because they are generally attracted to physical occupations, they love to demonstrate their techniques, tools, and methods. They prefer to show, not tell, others how to do something, and they are good leaders in any situation that requires physical exertion.

FINANCIAL CHOICES

Yellows tend to be childlike in their handling of finances. They trust that they will always be taken care of. They have an easy come, easy go attitude toward money. Rooted in their present wants and needs, Yellows don't worry much about future consequences. They can quickly spend to the limit on credit cards, forgetting that they will be responsible for paying it back.

Yellows see money as a vehicle to connect them to others in society. Money means a good time. Cars, clothes, and pocket money are the necessities of life for a Yellow. These are their tickets to where the action is: the bar, the beach, the ski slopes, any place where people congregate and have a good time.

Because of this attitude, Yellows do well when someone else handles their money. They may need automatic checking account deductions for loan payments, savings plans, retirement accounts, and whole life insurance policies. These services are perfect for Yellows, who are not good at remembering due dates on various payment plans. Ideally, Yellows operate well on a cash basis—no bookkeeping necessary! The mates of Yellows should handle the family finances, if possible. Yellows tend to overspend, running up large debts. They are reluctant to defer gratification for anything that is fun or satisfies their need for physical expression—sporting equipment, ski weekends, sexy new clothes. Yellows will cooperate if they understand and see the need for a financial program or budget, but they need frequent reminders. But be aware that to put a Yellow on a budget for a long period of time without regular updates on progress toward the goal will cause the Yellow to rebel out of resentment and lack of positive reinforcement, thereby sabotaging all the good work done up to that point. Therefore, a weekly review of financial planning strategies or decisions is essential for Yellows.

CAREER OPTIONS

Leadership ability is one of the major components of this Personality Spectrums color. This ability manifests itself when Yellows are working with a group of people in a team atmosphere. Yellows lead by assisting individuals in learning a skill or talent. They do well in any occupation that allows them to teach by demonstration, whether with tools, abilities, or techniques. As a result, they make good trainers, developers, teachers, and coaches.

They also make excellent supervisors or foremen because they first establish rapport with the people on the job. Once they have this rapport, they are able to use the force of their personality to entice and cajole people to work toward a common goal. They truly understand the nature of a winning ,team.

Yellows love being out of doors. Occupations such as forest ranger, construction worker, surveyor, police officer, landscape architect, and landscape maintenance person are all possibilities. They also make excellent salespeople because they love to be out and about, keeping their own schedule, meeting people, and sharing ideas. If they are selling a product, as opposed to an idea, Yellows love demonstrating its functions and capabilities.

If they can meet the demands of being in an office, Yellows

make wonderful travel agents because they will send their clients to all the places they would love to visit. They keep an ear open for unusual activities at bargain prices—and even if their clients don't like the activity, they won't be too mad, since the agent got it for them at a good rate. Yellows also make marvelous tour guides and excursion leaders. They are indefatigable, fearless, and adventuresome. If their clients can keep up with them, the Yellows will show them the time of their life.

SPIRITUALITY

Yellows understand spirituality in terms of God, a Higher Being that has created a world full of wonder. Spirituality for Yellows is neither an intellectual knowing nor an emotional experience. It is a physical sensation, an adrenaline rush. They are apt to describe it in statements such as "I felt God's hand on my shoulder" or "I felt as if I were being carried by a Higher Power." Yellows describe everything spiritual as a physical sensation, including theology and dogma. Seriousness does not appeal to Yellows. They are happiest in situations where they can easily and naturally express themselves. They want to wiggle, squirm, and jump up and down with the sheer physical joy of their spiritual experiences. Because of their physical needs, an active form of worship is most productive and satisfying for this Personality Spectrums color.

Yellows hold their spirituality with the innocence of children; they are hopeful, trusting, expectant. They see God in every butterfly, in every rainbow. Even as adults, Yellows greet the sunrise with emotional abandonment, thrilled with the possibilities of the new day. Yellows stand in awe of the physical perfection of the universe. As they see the world reflected in one drop of dew caught on a single filament of a spider's web, they ask, "How could there *not* be a Higher Power?" For Yellows, spirituality is the joy of being alive.

SEVEN

PHYSICAL TAN

Physical Tans are one of the three Eclipse Colors. An eclipse is different from an overlay. To have an eclipse in the aura means that the individual has two bands of color that completely surround the body, one outside the other. These two colors are interpreted as one color. This distinctive color pairing has its own character and personality style; it is not a marriage of the characteristics of the two colors that make up the combination. The two colors that make up Physical Tan are Mental Tan and Green. While Mental Tan and Green are both in the Mental Family of colors, the eclipse combination of the colors produces personality and character traits similar to those of the Yellow. Therefore, Physical Tan is one of the Physical (body) Personality Spectrums colors.

Physical Tans experience themselves as the physical center of the three-dimensional world that surrounds them. Their bodies behave like sonar sensing devices. They are constantly sending out signals and absorbing the echoes, translating the messages physically so that they can then process them mentally.

The strength of this color combination is that both components are independent, responsible, and willing to be their own authority. This means that people with this Eclipse Color tend to stand back and observe what is going on before they commit themselves. However, once committed, they are self-starters and initiators. They have a sense of their own individualism, which they hold as sacred.

The greatest challenge for a Physical Tan is to develop flexibility. Their experience of life has reinforced their belief that in order to be loved, they must perform according to other people's expectations. To a Physical Tan, this means that they must carry out a task, fulfill an agreement, or deliver a product before they can experience acceptance and love. This tends to make them rigid and inflexible in their expectations of themselves and others. By understanding their own nature, they can come to know that there is a place for them in life, where they will have autonomy within the system.

APPROACH TO PHYSICAL REALITY

Physical Tans, like Yellows, are part of the Physical (body) Family; their approach to life is primarily kinesthetic. For a Physical Tan, reality is three-dimensional; they must touch it, feel it, and operate in it to believe in it.

Physical Tans' perception of themselves as being in the center of a three-dimensional world is based not on egocentric arrogance but on the fact that they make sense out of their world by how they are positioned *in* it. This physical sensitivity means that they pick up on clues in the environment, clues that are dismissed by others. For example, Physical Tans who work as geologists have a sixth sense that helps them find what they are looking for. This know-how is based on their physical sensitivity, but they will use logic, data, maps, and contour drawings to document what they know in their bones. More practically, as Physical Tans enter a room, they react immediately, positioning themselves in one of several unique ways. When they feel crowded—confined mentally, emotionally, or physically—Physical Tans are apt to overreact by withdrawing emotionally, retreating physically, or shutting down socially. When physically uncomfortable, Physical Tans will get up abruptly and walk out of a room. They will exit even in the middle of a conversation; their reaction is so instinctive that they are usually unaware that they have been rude. This intense physical reaction is triggered by the emotionally based fear that they will not be in control of the situation.

Physical Tans, as a personality type, seem to stand between the world of the physical senses and the world of mental thoughts and processes. Their individual process is distinctly physical, with aspects that make them unmistakably different from the other Physical Personality Spectrums colors. Reds, for example, know that they can trust themselves in the world of the physical; Physical Tans are not sure. Physical Tans are cautious and deliberate when they take action; they lack the confidence the Reds have that they will prevail.

While Oranges are hedonistic in their pursuit of excitement and thrills, Physical Tans never put themselves in physical jeopardy for the thrill of it. They have too much respect for themselves and others to take foolish chances simply because the opportunity is there. Physical Tans approach risk from a more methodical, calculated point of view. The risk itself must stand for something; it must have a goal or purpose they consider worthy.

Magentas, with their uninhibited flamboyance, are willing to reorder and restructure the universe just to see what it might look like. Physical Tans, on the other hand, need to be able to count on their reality as being predictable and dependable, the same every day.

Physical Tans do not have the spontaneous, childlike joyfulness that is the hallmark of the Yellows. Physical Tans are much more self-controlled and reticent than the playful Yellow. Like Yellows, Physical Tans process everything through the physiology of their bodies. Physical Tans process through their musculature, which acts like a sonar device. Unlike Yellows who experience life as a biochemical high, Physical Tans experience life as a series of muscle-reflex reactions. As they tighten their muscles, they are reacting negatively to stress, demands, and expectations. As their muscles loosen, they experience physical and emotional flexibility and receptivity.

MENTAL ATTITUDES

This Personality Spectrums color makes decisions by handling or physically touching the tangible environment. When

Physical Tans need to know whether or not they have enough paper to finish a report, they pick up the stack of paper and mentally weigh it. Using their internal sonar system, Physical Tans orient themselves within physical space. They assign mental equivalents to things and people in their reality. They have a definitive spatial-relationship component that allows them to translate ideas into three-dimensional reality. This ability makes them excellent architects, inventory control personnel, purchasing agents, and city planners or developers.

Since their primary approach to life is kinesthetic—absorbing, analyzing, and processing the subtle cues in their material environment—they are keen observers, intent on gathering as much information as quickly as possible. They internalize this information; their body becomes a sensing device. As they absorb the data, they shift gears, analyzing mentally the components of the information they have received physically.

Like Mental Tans, Physical Tans have the capacity to be logical, sequential thinkers. Instead of dealing strictly with thoughts and ideas, as do the colors in the Mental Family, Physical tans process sensations, reducing them to objects and actions. The more concrete something can become, the better a Physical Tan can deal with it.

Physical Tans tend to be nonverbal. They have a difficult time translating what they sense through their bodies into words and concepts. They need to be taught how to draw analogies and develop ways of describing what they experience inside themselves. To make up for this lack of language, they learn the names of everything. As children, Physical Tans are absorbed in the activity of naming the things in their environment. If they can give an idea, feeling, or thing a name, then they are better able to deal with it. A name makes things real for a Physical Tan.

Physical Tans are relatively quiet as children, usually learning to talk late in their development. If allowed to absorb their environment of their own volition, they will begin the process of reporting their observations. They usually start speaking in full sentences at three years of age. Up until that time, they might not speak at all or do so only in single words, often causing their parents to fear that they are mentally retarded, hard of hearing, or suffering from some psychological dysfunction, such as autism. If dealt with lovingly by parents who are willing to constrain their own fears and show the child only encouragement and understanding, the Physical Tan child will learn to cut short the time lag between his or her physical process and the mental or emotional outcomes desired by family and friends. However, if a Physical Tan child is hounded by parents who make demands based on their own emotions and expectations, he or she will retreat inward, becoming less and less able to communicate satisfactorily. The individual may develop into an introspective, reticent adult who is unable and unwilling to accept criticism or participate in verbal give-and-take.

Physical Tans tend to be intelligent. Their verbal reticence is not a result of lack of mental ability or skills. But to develop their fine minds, they need to handle the physical environment—feeling it, touching it, and cataloging the inventory of their lives. The ability to see the possibility for changes, modify action plans, and switch tactics quickly is the gift this aura color has. Their greatest skill is like that of a military strategist. They are able to translate and project three-dimensional changes in reality.

This Personality Spectrums color pays meticulous attention to details. Things that are untidy, out of order, or in disarray make Physical Tans feel uncomfortable and unsafe. Unattended details are the emotional booby traps of their existence. Physical Tans tend to be very neat and tidy. They decide what to wear by touch, running their hands over their clothing. They clean the refrigerator to decide whether or not they need to go grocery shopping.

EMOTIONAL MAKEUP

Physical Tans are intensely private people. They do not readily express their emotions. That does not mean that Physical Tans are unfeeling—only that they do not have easy access to the verbal expression of their feelings.

They are slow to choose friends, tending to remain aloof in groups, carefully selecting those individuals with whom they feel safe enough to share their feelings. Physical Tans appear to be shy and reserved. But, instead, they are cautious and careful in opening up to other people. They do not invite others to enter their space. When ready, Physical Tans will make the first move, letting others know that their friendship will not be rejected. However, once engaged emotionally, Physical Tans are intensely involved. They develop a fierce loyalty to those with whom they feel emotionally safe.

Because they tend to be so private, Physical Tans are not willing to put their personal affections on display. Within a relationship, public demonstrations of affection are not common. Instead, they resort to secret code words or small gestures, such as a hand squeeze, that convey the warmth and meaning of the relationship to their mate. Once committed, Physical Tans assume that their love and devotion are accepted. They feel that public displays of affection are cheap imitations of the true depth of feelings, unworthy of the love and gratitude they feel for their partner. This private nature is, in fact, the greatest gift they bring to a relationship. Physical Tans, more than any other color, understand the true nature of intimacy.

They appear to be selfish and self-centered, as if they believe they are the center of the universe and give little thought or consideration to others. They often appear to be rude and thoughtless when, in fact, they have arrived at maximum sensory overload with little advance warning from their system. Their only perceived safety mechanism is to split, to leave the scene as quickly as possible. Yellows, on the other hand, leave a party or gathering because they sense that the group's vibrations are not compatible with theirs. Physical Tans pick up tension, but cannot name the feeling or anticipate the outcome. Like Yellows, they solve the problem by leaving.

For Physical Tans feelings are the third, and last, process they turn to in order to make sense out of the world, the first being their physical body and the second, their mind. Their full-time job is to learn to know themselves—to develop flexibility and patience with themselves. They need to learn a repertoire of emotional behaviors. This Personality Spectrums color, more than any other, has few emotional resources to draw on. Mental Tans can at least think they feel. Physical Tans, locked in their physical body, must first process everything kinesthetically. Once they understand and can name their physical sensations, they can convert their sensations to mental data and then translate that data to emotions, choosing behaviors and actions appropriate to the feeling side of their personality structure. Only when they have achieved some sense of their inner emotional landscape can they begin to venture outward, extending the boundaries to explore and understand the feeling expressions of others.

Physical Tans give the impression that they are emotionally unavailable. To some degree that is true. This reticence can be reinforced in childhood by critical, non-nurturing parents who cause them to retreat within themselves and to become unable, and later unwilling, to risk sharing any of their thoughts and feelings for fear of ridicule. Because the Physical Tans' approach is to sonar their way through life, parents who demand explanations of plans and actions may cause a Physical Tan to shut down emotionally. If Physical Tans are not able to learn to express their feelings in a loving, supportive environment, they can become introspective, rigid, unyielding adults, afraid to express their feelings for fear of being criticized.

SOCIAL STYLE

Physical Tans are extremely attractive individuals. Part of their charm lies in their elusiveness and their emotional aloofness. It is perceived as a challenge by those who would pursue them, thinking that they can entice a Physical Tan to warm up, let down their hair, and become emotionally available. Not so! Physical Tans are naturally shy and reserved. They need a time lag between receiving data and processing it. Pressure, either real or imagined, causes Physical Tans to withdraw even further, leaving their partner in the company of a body without a soul.

Physical Tans prefer to develop close friendships and relationships with people who exhibit self-sufficiency. Needy or dependent behaviors cause Physical Tans to withdraw first emotionally and then physically. They feel more comfortable helping those who can help themselves, so that they do not feel wholly responsible for the outcome.

Friends and mates must be willing to give a Physical Tan plenty of personal space as well as physical and emotional freedom. This will win the Physical Tan's loyalty, trust, gratitude, and ultimately love. For mates to give a Physical Tan emotional freedom means to allow them time to process their facts into sensations and then to translate those sensations into feelings. Once they feel emotionally safe, they prefer to have their sexual needs met where their emotional needs are lovingly handled. It is as if Physical Tans seek, through sexual liaisons, the nurturing and emotional understanding they desire. Once their emotional needs are met, they place high value on fidelity, which is consistent with their concept of loyalty.

COMPATIBILITY WITH OTHER COLORS

Physical (environmental) Colors

Reds and Physical Tans share a healthy appetite for lusty sexual experiences coupled with a strong awareness of their physical surroundings and environment. These two colors, when they act in concert for a common cause, can create a powerful physical and emotional attraction. This is a color combination that gets things done.

Oranges are too fiercely independent to be good mates to Physical Tans. Neither of these colors is willing to give an inch emotionally or physically to the other. Any relationship between them ends in a stalemate.

Physical Tans regard Magentas as the peacocks of the spectrum, making a lot of noise and attracting attention to themselves. A Physical Tan is not comfortable sharing the limelight with this noisy, zany bird. The Physical Tan requires a more subdued partner.

Physical (body) Colors

Yellows revive in Physical Tans the hope that people are trustworthy and friendly; they are like sunshine in a Physical Tan's life. However, the Yellows' immaturity and heedless quest for good times and fun can try the patience of the more sedate, serious Physical Tan.

Physical Tans mated to Physical Tans can experience serious communication problems. If they are not willing to open up and express their innermost emotions, they enter an intimate relationship with a serious disadvantage. This inability to share emotions effectively could make them better business partners than marriage partners.

Mental Colors

Mental Tans tend to reinforce the cautious streak in the Physical Tan. Because they are both so particular about details, their relationship can get bogged down in trivia.

Greens and Physical Tans are a dynamic twosome. The quicksilver agility of a Green mind entrances and enchants a Physical Tan. Physical Tans have a litheness and grace that excites a Green. Mentally and sexually this is an exciting pair.

Nurturing Tans tend to be too compliant to suit the needs of a Physical Tan. Also, a Nurturing Tan who does not have a firm grasp on his or her own identity can easily get swallowed up by the emotional and physical needs of the Physical Tan.

Loving Tans, with their habit of littering their environment with their possessions, would drive the Physical Tans crazy. The Physical Tans' penchant for order and neatness would cause stress within the relationship. Loving Tans are much more haphazard about everything in life. Physical Tans do not leave anything to chance. A relationship between these two colors would be an emotional and mental challenge.

Emotional/Spiritual Colors

Blues would have to be very strong and determined to be able to hold their own emotionally in relationships with Physical Tans. In their attempt to meet the needs of everyone—

mate, children, in-laws, employers—Blues will end up not pleasing anyone, especially their Physical Tan mate. Physical Tans need to know that they come first in the relationship. And with a Blue, that is not always possible.

Violets have personal power comparable to that of a Physical Tan. Therefore, in a relationship they cannot be browbeaten or intimidated by either the silences or the quiet rage of a Physical Tan. Violets are able first to set firm limits and boundaries within the relationship and then to fall into bed and make intense love with their Physical Tan mate.

Lavenders are intimidated by Physical Tans, whose power, confidence, and physicality tend to overwhelm and awe a Lavender. While attracted to their powerful sexuality, a Lavender does not feel emotionally safe or psychically secure with a Physical Tan. The relationship is one that would do better in the realm of fantasy than in the world of reality.

Crystals and Physical Tans have nothing in common. Crystals live within themselves. Physical Tans live in the world. While both these colors are looking for a home that will be a quiet haven and retreat from the world, each wants the other to create it.

Indigos are an enigma to Physical Tans. Indigos perceive themselves to be a law unto themselves; they are unwilling to be dictated to by others. Physical Tans have a difficult time relating to that kind of independent thought in others. Instead of a relationship filled with love and mutual respect, this can become one of domination and control on one side and indifference on the other.

PERSONAL POWER AND LEADERSHIP STYLE

Physical Tans have a strong sense of individuality, self-possession, and control that others often mistake for leadership ability. In truth, what they have is the ability to be meticulous in following orders and to be devoted to a cause. They are practical and have a strong belief in the chain of command. While they lack many of the traits that make for true leadership—charisma, compassion, and communication skills—they are loyal, faithful, single-minded, and fearless, and they can separate their emotions from their actions.

Physical Tans tend to be loners. Camaraderie and socializing are not activities they especially enjoy. They are perceived to be aloof and standoffish by their peer group, hard to get to know and sometimes hard to like. When forced to socialize, they often drink too much in the hope that the alcohol will loosen them up. Instead, all it does is to drive them deeper into their reserve of self-control. Because Physical Tans have such literal minds, they have difficulty telling jokes, making puns, and indulging in wordplay. This severely hampers them from joining in group banter at parties and social functions. On the job, they are at a disadvantage when competing with more personable candidates for promotions and leadership opportunities. Physical Tans only want to be recognized for the tangible contribution they make, not for their social skills.

FINANCIAL CHOICES

Money, to a Physical Tan, is a thing. In its abstract forms, it is an intangible that Physical Tans do not understand. For them, the issue is *security*. They understand the physicality of the things that money can buy. Physical Tans think of purchases as investments—whether it is the clothes they wear or the automobiles they drive. They do not speculate; they do not trust fluctuating interest rates or other market indicators. High-risk stocks, speculative investments, and other get-rich-quick schemes do not appeal to them.

They are practical and down to earth in their personal style and taste. They prefer possessions designed for function rather than style, ease over elegance. Because this Personality Spectrums color is so tactile, Physical Tans tend to make decisions based on weight; they prefer a sturdy chair that cannot be easily tipped over to lightweight decorator models. The key words they look for in advertising are "solid," "dependable," and "long-lasting." They want to know that they have made a good choice. They spend money cautiously. They listen to sales pitches, read *Consumer Reports,* and comparison-shop. They seldom indulge in impulse buying. They go shopping armed with a list. They concentrate on the task at hand and complete it as quickly as possible. Crowds and stores put all of this aura color's sensors on notice. Trinkets, baubles, or fads have little meaning to a Physical Tan because of their transitory nature. A Physical Tan notices the quality, durability, and craftsmanship of a product.

They are pragmatic when dealing with money. Physical Tans are very literal about finances, personal spending, and income. They understand borrowing for the purpose of buying a home or a business. Borrowing to pay for a vacation makes no sense to them; however, using discretionary income or saving for one does. They have a strong work ethic and are willing to forgo the short-term goal for the deferred gratification of a long-term goal, although they sometimes forget why they are working so hard.

CAREER OPTIONS

Physical Tans are the strategists; they make things happen when physical movement is required. Occupations or activities requiring the ability to project logistically, to manipulate supply lines, to deploy personnel and machinery, to map out the strategy of complex operations maneuvers, or to acquire leverage are all skills inherent to this Personality Spectrums color.

Physical Tans are above all tactile. Their well-defined sense of spatial relationships allows them to do well in occupations such as warehousing, inventory control, and shipping and receiving. They can also use these same skills in sports such as tennis, polo, hockey, and football. In each case, players must make judgments about the next move based on information received through their hands. They must translate that information so as to move the puck or ball through a physical maze to a predetermined goal. Because of their cool-headedness under pressure, Physical Tans do well in professional sports.

Physical Tans also do well in the military. The attributes that are so characteristic of a Physical Tan—loyalty, perseverance, dedication, order, and determination—are prized by the military. Physical Tans are usually attracted to special forces units that require independence and resourcefulness. They also make excellent troubleshooters for industries. Physical Tans can handle a strenuous travel schedule well, while being able to maintain their independence on the job.

SPIRITUALITY

Spirituality is a very private thing for Physical Tans. The spiritual experience for a Physical Tan, as for a Yellow, is a physical sensation. The difference is that a Physical Tan experiences a quiet, inner sense of peace and well-being whereas the Yellow experiences a rush of exhilaration or ecstasy. For a Physical Tan to publicly talk about a spiritual experience is to tarnish it, dissipating the energy and good feeling in unnecessary discussion. Physical Tans are the most introspective of all the Personality Spectrums colors; they must first sort through a complex structure of feelings before they can put words to their belief system. It may take Physical Tans years to digest a spiritual concept sufficiently in order to be able to explain it to themselves or share it with others. Abrupt changes and adjustments in spiritual habits or practices by the family or social group can cause fearfulness and rebellion within a Physical Tan. Such a rupture at this deep level of their being causes them to withdraw into themselves, denying themselves an opportunity to explore their belief system by getting some outside feedback.

Physical Tans hold the Higher Being and the President in somewhat the same category: as Commander-in-Chief of their respective areas. They recognize, and are obedient to, the concept of an organizing principle larger than themselves. However, they are unable to translate their spiritual experiences into an understanding of human experience. For them, the deep strata accessed only by spiritual experiences remain separated from the other levels of meaning in their lives. Once Physical Tans accept a theology or belief system, they appear to follow it tenaciously. This is a misconception, because Physical Tans never accept anything on faith or trust alone. What might be interpreted as rigid adherence to a set of beliefs is the Physical Tan's inability to translate the belief system into a set of feelings or words. Therefore, spirituality is a thing apart for them.

They can appear to be rigid and unyielding in their outlook and evaluation. Based on the way they experience the spiritual, Physical Tans think their experience is the *only* experience. When they try to impose their beliefs or rituals on others without being able to explain the purpose or meaning behind such adherence, they unwittingly substitute the shell for the substance of soul. Physical Tans lack the verbal skills to describe those deep, emotional moments of illumination when their souls have been touched. Because they are unable to explain these deep feelings, they unknowingly deprive others of a beacon to mark their spiritual knowledge and experience.

For a Physical Tan, *place* is an integral and necessary part of spirituality. This is the aura color on whom ancient holy places have a profound impact. Sedona, Machu Picchu, Stonehenge, Mecca—the energy in these places and the pilgrims who visit them speaks powerfully and directly to the souls of Physical Tans. As they stand before the high altars of the world's religions, they sense the millennia of prayers that have made their way heavenward. The profoundness of such faith speaks powerfully to the soul of a Physical Tan.

EIGHT

MENTAL TAN

The key to happiness and success for Mental Tans is understanding the process of intuition. They must journey from cold logic into the unknown of metaphysics. They can accomplish this task only if they are willing to become risk-takers. Part of this journey involves learning to leap from the position of physical, mental, and emotional safety into the realm of the unknown. This means having faith and trusting their intuition.

In order to be able to let go of the safe and secure, Mental Tans must recognize that their feelings and emotions are the gateway to intuition. They can gain access to the realm of hunches only by getting in touch with and feeling those emotions. They need to learn how to express their feelings authentically without trying to rationalize them away. As they relinquish their "need to know," larger and larger possibilities open up to them. They begin to understand that the leap of faith is not a free fall into disaster and chaos.

APPROACH TO PHYSICAL REALITY

Mental Tans primarily use their minds in dealing with reality instead of relying on bodily sensations or other physical cues. They tend to see things first as an idea: while they understand and appreciate nature, sex, the smell of a new baby, they think about it first as an abstraction. Later they put

101

an action to the thought—for example, by thinking of how much they love someone and then deciding to actually make love.

Mental Tans see all aspects of daily life as a complex whole just waiting to be disassembled into its component parts. Breakfast is not a meal, but rather a combination of the specific and unchanging foods and drinks that constitute the concept of breakfast. Therefore, non–breakfast items such as asparagus and caviar do not belong on the breakfast table. Mental Tans don't perceive themselves as rigid or inflexible; rather their outer reality—the breakfast table—must conform to the idea they carry around in their heads.

Because they tend to spend so much time in their heads, Mental Tans are not much interested in physical reality except as an interesting abstraction. They love knowing how and why something works, and they will use infinite patience to take something apart and put it back together again.

They are curious about the mechanics of how the real world works. They see and comprehend the vast variety of products, goods, and services; they just don't see the need for them. But beyond that, they would just as soon not bother with all the decisions that need to be made about all those choices. To them, one house is essentially the same as another, one item of apparel just as good as another. They ask, "Why should I own two sweaters when I can only wear one at a time?"

This attitude holds true except where new ideas are embodied in mechanical devices such as computers, tools, photography equipment, or appliances. Mental Tans will have the newest and latest model of each. To them, the engineering concepts inherent in each invention are marvels to behold. It is not unusual for Mental Tans to own several computer systems, each an improvement over the last, designed to work faster and better and to do more work or run more programs. And they are reluctant to part with systems that have become obsolete because they think of them as old, trusted friends.

Health and physical fitness for a Mental Tan are not just a matter of diet and exercise but an excuse to create some sort of statistical profile for the purpose of analyzing weight and inches lost, miles run, foods eaten, and vitamins taken. Exercise is seldom done just to enjoy the out-of-doors, but rather because it fits with a particular regimen's recommendation. Mental Tans' relationship to physical reality comes as a result of their thinking process.

MENTAL ATTITUDES

Mental Tans are among those Personality Spectrums colors who get their pleasure and creativity from interacting with others on an intellectual level. They love to think, play with ideas, and organize systems, and are happiest when able to mentally grasp and manipulate the environment by means of ideas and the thinking process.

Mental Tans' major function, until the advent of the computer, was that of data keeper of society. They are fascinated with the details, the complex puzzle pieces of life. They want to filter the world through their minds and process the information until every piece of the puzzle is in place, with nothing left over and nothing left out.

The Mental Tans' greatest asset is their ability to reason logically, to figure things out, not as problem solvers but rather like systems analysts or like a CPA doing an audit. Their mental process is sequential and orderly. They carefully think each idea through one step at a time in an orderly and sequential manner—as in steps 1, 2, 3, 4, 5, 6, 7, 8, 9, 10—without skipping ahead or using shortcuts.

They love processes such as long division, which have a regular pattern. They like writing down all their mental work on a piece of paper, making sure every part of step 1 is complete before moving to step 2 in order to see that each part

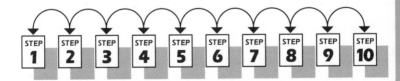

of the problem or challenge is neatly accounted for before advancing to the next stage. Mental Tans like to be able to go back and double-check their work if anything should go wrong once they reach step 10.

Though methodical, meticulous, and painstaking in their attention to detail, they often make decisions clinically, without considering the emotions or sentiments of the people involved. Mental Tan are naturals for careers and positions that require a kind of ruthless conscientiousness.

Problems sometimes arise when Mental Tans need to go beyond their accumulated data base in order to make an educated guess. Mental Tans may even cheat by seeking to validate the educated guess with reams of additional data. To avoid an intuitive solution, a Mental Tan will retreat into a familiar pattern, solving the same type of problem over and over in an attempt to convince themselves that they are, in fact, working on a new situation. The Mental Tan must make the mental and emotional stretch in order to get beyond this need to know, to try something new for which there are no hard data, no guarantee of success. This is the leap of faith they must make, and it begins when they acknowledge the need to take risks.

Once they have faced risk and gained confidence in their abilities, this is the Personality Spectrums color most able to assess the risks involved in any decision-making process. However, in assessing those risks, Mental Tans open themselves again to the endless weighing and measuring inherent in the step-by-step process.

EMOTIONAL MAKEUP

Personal growth and development for a Mental Tan hinges on handling and dealing with feelings and emotions. Mental Tans want to recognize and make sense out of sentiments, reducing the resulting behavior to that of logic. They are uncomfortable with anything they do not understand or cannot control. They want to reduce all of life's situations, including interpersonal relationships, to mathematical equations to be solved by analyzing and depersonalizing human emotion. They want to organize their feelings and those of others.

Because they want to discount emotions and to pretend that they are separate from the logical, mental process, Mental Tans may seem cold and dispassionate. They are often heard to say, "I think I feel . . ."

When they don't know what to do with their own emotions, they tend to ignore the emotions of others, pretending that feelings do not exist. Having to take into consideration the attitudes, beliefs, and values of others disrupts the logical process for a Mental Tan.

Individuals of this aura color look for problem-solving models in the field of mechanical engineering. However, feelings and emotions are not neat and tidy; they are not predictable and often spring from hurts and angers buried deep within an individual's psyche.

The greatest challenge that Mental Tans must confront is dealing with their own emotions. Because they try to keep feelings separate from their mental process, Mental Tans tend to appear hard, cold, unemotional, and uninvolved. But occasionally their own pent-up emotions get out of control. Then Mental Tans express them as anger or rage, which is manifested in dramatic and startling behaviors such as table-pounding, door-slamming, or outbursts of temper. Conversely, they may become depressed, turning the rage and anger inward, withdrawing emotionally from family and friends, becoming hypercritical or uncommunicative. This internalized rage can also manifest itself as an alcohol or drug problem or as a health problem like high blood pressure, ulcers, or a heart condition.

The challenge for a Mental Tan, then, is to learn to get in touch with and to express their moods and sentiments regularly in ways that encourage communication and understanding. They need to learn when to integrate their emotions into their decision-making process. The best way for them to do this is to start by sorting through all the data logically and making a tentative decision. They should then consider their own and others' feelings, as the basis for making their final decision. When they have learned to trust their feelings, Mental Tans can make the leap from the known, across the void of the unknown, and safely arrive at the end result.

Feelings are the gateway to the Mental Tans' intuition; but before they can release access to their intuitive powers they must gain access to their emotions. They must make a leap of faith and a flight of intuition. This requires that they learn to trust themselves and others. Mental Tans hesitate to take that leap for fear that they might be wrong. As they allow themselves to experience their own intuition, they will be able to understand that there is something just as important as logic, which then opens the gates to the exciting realm of their own creative process.

SOCIAL STYLE

Mental Tans embody the masculine energy components of initiative, drive, and direction. Thus, for them, social situations need to have a purpose or a function. Even then, Mental Tans have difficulty relaxing and having a good time. This Personality Spectrums color is not frivolous. A part of them feels that having a good time is a waste of time. Therefore, they join professional or service organizations for the purpose of combining social interactions with business. In addition, they tend to like groups where interaction is less intense and less intimate.

For Mental Tans, social life is much narrower in focus than for many of the other colors. They prefer quiet time where they can read or tinker rather than talk. They have so much going on in their heads that unless others share their interests the conversation can be boring to both parties. Mental Tans are not interested in what others are thinking—unless it happens to be the same thing they are thinking. Polite small talk is not their forte.

They seem to stand aloof from deep personal involvement, even in their love relationships. Mental Tans commit themselves deeply but have little capacity for spiritual or emotional intimacy. Mental Tans tend to marry for companionship and caretaking rather than for deep passion or intimacy. Fondness and deep caring for mates is typical of a Mental Tan's response to love and marriage. It is as if, once the ceremony is over, they can heave a sigh of relief that that little detail has been taken care of and they can get back to the really important things in life—their work and their ideas. Mental Tans, male and female, understand better than any other color the value of the role of helpmeet. But problems can arise when they fail to recognize and respond to their partner's desire or need for more attention. They often try to figure out logically what went wrong, responding to the situation from the mental point of view rather than understanding the deep longings and desires that their mates are attempting to express. They often take a workshop or seminar hoping to find a panacea to remedy the situation. Instead, they need to understand that there has to be a shift at the emotional level, which will require a whole new set of attitudes and behaviors on the part of the Mental Tan. Mental Tans need to get in touch with their feelings, not as an intellectual exercise, but as a genuine response to emotions.

COMPATIBILITY WITH OTHER COLORS

Physical (environmental) Colors

The Physical (environmental) Colors tend to find the Mental Tans stodgy and stuffy.

Reds want to get down and get funky, while Mental Tans want to think it over and decide if that is the best course of action under the circumstances. However, beneath their intellectual facade, Mental Tans recognize and appreciate the drive and determination that are so much a part of a Red's personality.

Oranges want to do their own thing uninhibited by others standing on the sidelines wringing their hands and worrying. Mental Tans have a difficult time understanding such strong independence.

Magentas consider Mental Tans too dull for words. There would be little compatibility between a Mental Tan and a Magenta unless the Mental Tan had figured how to set aside the "little professor" aspect of their personality and to look at the world through 3-D glasses.

Physical (body) Colors

Yellows, with their innocent playfulness, could coax a Mental Tan out to play, especially if the activity involved using analytical skills. A Yellow would help to keep a Mental Tan young and physically fit.

In a relationship between a Physical Tan and a Mental Tan practical considerations would take precedence over emotions or feelings. Bank accounts would be balanced, investments would be wisely handled, and a complete inventory of all possessions would be on hand. A problem would arise in that neither partner would know how to open up and maintain communications.

Mental Colors

A Mental Tan mated with a Mental Tan would remind their friends and family of Grant Wood's painting, *American Gothic*. Duty, honor, and commitment would be the hallmarks of this relationship.

A Green would provide the mental stimulus so necessary for the inner health of a Mental Tan. However, because Greens tend to skip ahead intellectually, they become impatient with the pedantic and prosaic thought processes of the Mental Tan, and this can lead to emotional conflicts.

Nurturing Tans think like Mental Tans and listen with their hearts; therefore, this could be a very compatible combination creating a stable, permanent relationship.

The random thought process that characterizes the Loving Tan causes the Mental Tan amusement and disbelief. The Loving Tan loves the methodical, step-by-step process of the Mental Tan, but the scattered thinking of a Loving Tan creates discomfort for a Mental Tan.

Emotional/Spiritual Colors

In general, Blues are the one Personality Spectrums color with the emotional makeup to interact successfully with a Mental Tan. Blue is predominantly a woman's color, and these women are perceived as the perfect wives and mothers. As long as they are willing to fulfill that role, the relationship will function well for both parties. However, when the Blue wants to grow and has no words to explain the frustration and helplessness, the Mental Tan will want to fix a situation that cannot be fixed. Inner fears and self-doubt will cause the Mental Tan to withdraw.

Violets, with their capacity to see the long-term outcome, help a Mental Tan to keep moving and not get stuck in the details of life. Violets are more willing to take risks and thus assist Mental Tans in making their leap of faith.

Lavenders tend to find Mental Tans too pedantic to be much fun. Lavenders want to escape into a fantasy vacation and Mental Tans want to know the name, address, and telephone number of the hotel to leave in case of emergency. However tedious Lavenders may find the Mental Tans' thinking process, they are amazed at the tenacity with which the Mental Tans question and probe the nature of their own minds.

Crystals are usually seen as possessions by their Mental Tan mates and lovers because their beauty and personality seem so fragile and brittle. Therefore, Mental Tans tend to be too much in awe of Crystals to have warm, interactive relationships with them.

Indigos are not grounded enough to appeal to a Mental Tan over the long term. Their vagueness, inability to make a commitment, and unwillingness to become another's possession keep these colors apart.

PERSONAL POWER AND LEADERSHIP STYLE

Mental Tans are one of the Leadership Colors. Their leadership technique is to include others in the fact-finding aspects of the decision-making process. As middle managers, when presented with a problem, they poll their people for ideas and insights on all facets of the situation. Their motto is "Come, let us reason together." Their teams appreciate this management style and give loyalty and service in exchange for an opportunity to be listened to. However, Mental Tans are not swayed by the opinions or feelings of those who work for them. Instead, they listen carefully, take all of the data presented to them, organize it, and analyze it, but they reserve the right to make the final decision themselves.

Loyal, hardworking, and dedicated to their job commitments, Mental Tans make excellent middle managers because they are the conduit through which information flows from bottom to top and top to bottom within an organization. Their personal strength is in their ability to pay attention to the details that most other colors ignore or don't notice. They take pride in a job well done, no matter how boring or unexciting it may be. When asked how they can stand such a boring job, they reply that they don't find it boring, that someone has to do it, and so that someone might as well be them.

FINANCIAL CHOICES

Mental Tans, who seem so unemotional about everything else in life, can become very emotional when it comes to money and financial matters. In personal relationships, this causes a great deal of confusion, hurt, and anger. The reason for this apparent inconsistency in a Mental Tan's personality is that they are very security-conscious. Money is the one thing that Mental Tans cannot predict and control through logical means. Therefore, their attitude toward it is one of caution, skepticism, and distrust. All money decisions are made with great fear and trepidation. Everything else is chancy. They see their paycheck as the only thing standing between their life-style and destitution. Anything that endangers or alters the status quo causes them to feel panic—releasing feelings of fear and anticipated loss. Rather than admit these feelings, Mental Tans will cover their insecurity with arguments and tirades against rising prices, government controls, frivolous spending habits, and the moral decline of society.

Because they are so security-conscious, Mental Tans do not make decisions regarding money quickly. Each and every option must be subjected to excruciatingly minute analysis before a Mental Tan will, reluctantly, make a decision. Mental Tans do not seem to be able to take risks with money. Whenever the potential loss is greater than the potential gain, Mental Tans will choose the safer financial option.

Mental Tans do not seem to be creative in the ways they earn money, either. They are stuck in the conventional ways of making money: working for a salary or paycheck, sticking to saving accounts, pension plans, and real-estate investments. Those investments include owning a home and perhaps one or two income properties that provide something to tinker around with. The stock portfolio is a balanced combination of blue chips and municipal bonds, which the Mental Tan follows religiously on the stock pages of the newspapers. All other investment opportunities are unacceptable to a Mental Tan.

CAREER OPTIONS

As a result of their ability to pay attention to details, Mental Tans excel at jobs and careers in which painstaking attention to details will lead to success. Such careers include accounting, law, civil service, data entry, computer programming, engineering, small-appliance repair, purchasing, inventory control, and some fields of medicine such as radiology.

Because they work well with people, they do well in middle management positions where supervision, problem-solving, and production are the outcomes. As teachers, they are thorough, methodical, and by-the-book. They convey information in a conceptual framework, usually in accordance with the scope and sequence of the educational system's guidelines.

SPIRITUALITY

Spirituality for a Mental Tan is the study of the higher order of the universe and the laws and principles that govern it. Mental Tans want to understand the mental constructs, the laws or probabilities that create order out of spiritual chaos. The concept of a God, a Higher Power, eludes the Mental Tans. They can define it, read about it, think about it, but they have difficulty feeling it. Mental Tans want to think their way logically to spirituality. They see the miracle of creation as a mystery to be solved, an equation to be understood.

Accordingly, they most often find themselves at home in religions that offer a code of laws, rules, or regulations. They hope that adherence to the form will be the key that will open the recesses of their hearts. In hoping to gain access to the concept of God through form, Mental Tans tend to become rigid and set in their ways. They are afraid that if they disturb the form, they will destroy their chance of knowing God.

They are seldom carried to the heights of ecstasy in their spiritual quest. Mental Tans consider emotionalism in religion a cheap high. They are unwilling to recognize the deep layers of the soul that some lay bare to God at those alchemical spiritual moments. Instead, they may see spirituality as synonymous with duty, justice, and honor. As Mental Tans live according to these religious values, they achieve peace, order, and dependability, which for them are the hallmarks of a life well lived.

NINE

GREEN

Intellectually intense, and able to pare an idea to the bone—these are attributes of an analytical Green. Greens measure their own worth by their ability to be *productive,* generating countless ideas and projects, and by their *creative* ability, which allows them to devise innovative, workable solutions to problems. They are the planners, organizers, and strategists of the Personality Spectrums.

Their greatest fear is that what they create and produce will not be good enough and they will be found lacking. This low sense of self-esteem leads Greens into an emotional box canyon where being perfect is seen as necessary to earn the love and respect of those around them. The major lesson that all Greens must learn is that life can be easy, elegant, and fun, but if they wish to live that kind of life, they must give up their emotional need to be perfect.

APPROACH TO PHYSICAL REALITY

Greens are mental. Their response to life's challenges is to think about them. In other words, they deal with physical reality in an offhand way, giving it due consideration, but not dwelling on the exigencies of a given situation. Greens would rather devise a solution to a problem than get in and *do* something about it. Greens think abstractly and analytically; when faced with situations that require hard physical labor, Greens hire other people to do the work.

Greens' relationship to the world of things is one of remote viewing. They see many situations as problems to be solved. Even when they are preparing for a party or organizing a move, they tend to operate from a distance—directing others where to put the chairs or on which table to set the centerpiece. Even if Greens actually have to do the work themselves, they seem detached and emotionally uninvolved from what is going on.

Physical reality does not seem to have much meaning for Greens. In the evolutionary unfolding of a physical event from seed to shoots, leaves, flower, and a finally dead stalk, Greens see the dead stalk in the seed, bypassing all the intervening stages. Because their minds are so agitated when faced with stagnation, Greens leap to outcomes and solutions whereas other Personality Spectrums colors find meaning and joy in the process itself. Everything Greens do, from perusing art to purchasing clothing, is done with an eye toward efficiency and expediency and with little wasted time or motion.

Greens dislike hard physical labor, and their contribution is most often mental rather than physical. For example, Greens will spend long hours working on ideas, plans, and projections. They prefer working harder to pay others to maintain their homes and automobiles and to create beautifully catered meals. They see these tasks as boring drudgery lacking in originality.

MENTAL ATTITUDES

Green is the second of the Mental Family of Personality Spectrums colors. Greens are intelligent, quick-witted, rational, and logical, but they must be productive to be happy. They see life as a giant "to do" list, and they will happily check off all of the tasks they have completed. Nothing satisfies Greens more than a day in which they have accomplished everything they set out to do.

Greens are naturally ingenious, constantly rearranging the pieces of information within their minds, searching for new combinations and patterns. This activity renews them, giving them a sense of freshness about themselves and the world. A problem can arise, however, from a Green's certainty that all mental activity must serve some productive end, with a concrete goal in sight, instead of being valued for itself. To create as a form of play is one of the hardest lessons for a Green to learn.

Greens look upon life as a puzzle to be solved, and they enjoy the pursuit of solutions. They are happiest when they arrive at conclusions or explanations. Ambiguous ideas and undertakings left unfinished cause Greens mental and emotional uneasiness. This is where they often compensate by insisting on being productive.

The thinking pattern of a Green is similar to that of a Mental Tan; it is logical, sequential, and orderly. The important difference between them is that while Mental Tans process information step by step (1, 2, 3, 4, 5, 6, 7, 8, 9, 10), Greens

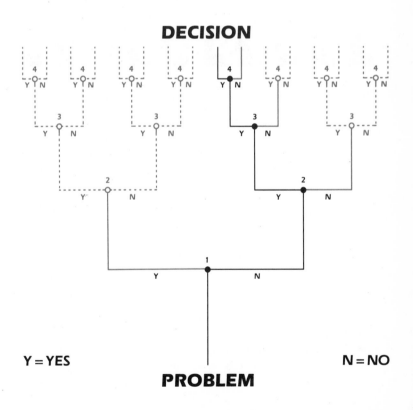

DECISION

Y = YES   N = NO

PROBLEM

think in a binary fashion, considering possibility A as opposed to option B. Once a decision has been made, then one whole pathway of options is closed down. Greens are constantly paring away options that require too much work, do not produce results, or lead in unproductive directions.

When Greens try to communicate with other colors who do not use this analytical process, a problem arises when a single alternative can lead to more than one consequence. Many different ideas can be generated from the first two steps, but Greens consider only one path to the goal. Breakdowns in communication can occur when a Green has settled on a solution and others are still discussing the original alternative.

* OC = OUTCOME

Greens can also work backwards. State the solution or result desired, and a Green will mentally stand at the goal, imagine what it took to get there, and then reconstruct the steps to the solution. However, no Green wants to stick around and do all the work involved in making a project come alive. Once the procedure has been identified, Greens want to move to the next good idea. They do not like to follow through on the details.

Greens are versatile thinkers. Because they can see patterns and recognize the structure, given a sample of information, they are able to determine the order or sequence represented by the data. Thus, they are able to identify behavior patterns, categories, or hierarchies based on very little information. This skill is useful in coordinating group work.

EMOTIONAL MAKEUP

Creative problem-solving is the primary outlet for Greens. Too often, however, Greens become stuck in the productive aspect of their color and neglect their creative urges. Greens regard creativity as a form of goofing off or just having fun. The challenge for Greens is to find the balance between the productive, result-oriented side of their nature and the creative, spontaneous aspect of themselves.

It is difficult for Greens to feel at an emotional level and to process their emotions. They know there is a sensible result waiting for them at step 10; however, they frequently rush the process to avoid experiencing the emotions. When they feel frightened, out of control, or emotionally threatened, they become compulsive, controlling, and rigid in their behavior. All these responses are safety mechanisms they have developed in order to reestablish their emotional balance and make sense out of the situation. When Greens lose control of a situation, or of their lives, they often threaten to commit suicide as a method of regaining their hold on things.

Greens need someone with whom they can discuss ideas. A relationship with an intellectually compatible partner is a priority for them. Essentially, Greens are more interested in ideas than they are in people. Once they understand that they are appreciated and valued by others for their minds, however, they open up and become warm, exciting people to be with.

SOCIAL STYLE

Because Greens are primarily interested in ideas, they are sexually attracted to those who admire them for their fine mind. Once they feel sure that they are not seen as just a physical plaything, they become physically and emotionally available to their partner. It is only when Greens feel appreciated mentally that they can make an emotional commitment. Because Greens can separate their emotions from their minds, however, they can become physically involved without becoming emotionally attached.

Greens marry mainly for mental stimulation and intellectual companionship. Home, children, and financial security are incidental. Allowed to follow their own internal timing, Greens tend to marry later in life and to have few or no children, preferring to commit themselves to well-established careers.

By nature, Greens are not nurturers, but in our society, Greens have had to adapt themselves to raising children and managing a home. They tend to be organizational parents, making sure the child has many opportunities for educational and physical development. They are willing to work extra hours to pay for piano lessons, uniforms, or tuition.

Greens resent emotional ties and demands placed on them by spouses and children. They therefore do best in small families with one or two children. Greens' children are usually bright and intelligent because the parents discuss ideas with them and encourage their intellectual development.

In social situations, Greens tend to be the observers. They often stand apart, waiting for someone else to make the first move. Greens are not wallflowers, although they are seldom outgoing or make the warm or compassionate gesture. They never join a group just to be part of it. They respond to social situations with ideas rather than feelings. Because they are so mental, they tend to be loners, choosing their closest friends carefully and giving much thought and deliberation to those alliances.

Personal relationships with Greens can be a challenge. Because they are so agile mentally, they usually have the answer first. This ability to leap quickly from idea to idea antagonizes co-workers and loved ones. Greens are seen as more interested in the product than the process. Others get their feelings hurt because the Greens' need to achieve resolution tends to discount the value of teamwork. Greens who are bored and waiting for everyone else to catch up are perceived by others as impatient and irritable, which, in fact, they are.

COMPATIBILITY WITH OTHER COLORS

Physical (environmental) Colors

Greens find the colors in the Physical (environmental) group fascinating and challenging. Their physicality provides an interesting balance to the Greens' strong mental component. The strong, fun-loving, lust of a Red provides a nice counterpoint to the cerebral gyrations of the Green. This can be a dynamic partnership if both parties deal honestly and respectfully with the other's strengths.

Greens see Oranges as a challenge, a dare. Greens sometimes feel that they can outthink any color in the spectrum. They try to control others by jumping ahead intellectually to cut them off at the pass. Oranges are equally unwilling to compromise. They try to control the relationship by refusing to give their allegiance to anyone.

Magentas have many of the same mental characteristics as Greens. However, instead of creating constructs within the mind as a Green does, Magentas construct them in three-dimensional reality. Though the processes are the same, the medium is different. There is a rich compatibility between these two colors.

Physical (body) Colors

Greens find the innocent childlike Yellow too saccharine for their tastes. Greens love sophistication, elegance, and style. Yellows much prefer hot dogs and apple pie. However, if Greens are willing to let down the barriers and play, they could not ask for a more loving playmate.

Physical Tans and Greens have an instant chemistry. The sparks of sexual electricity can be felt throughout the room the moment these two colors come together. The aloofness of the Physical Tan ignites the spark of challenge in the Green, and all of the highly refined mental abilities of the Green are brought into action to attract, lure, and capture the heart of the Physical Tan.

Mental Colors

Mental Tans and Greens have much in common and are often interested in the same leisure activities, subjects, and books. This is a relationship founded on common ground, driven by mutual respect and teamwork, and accepted by both as a marvelous solution to a tricky situation, divorce statistics being what they are. Problems can arise if the two do not appreciate and understand each other's way of thinking. Because Mental Tans are more methodical thinkers, they can be perceived as pedantic and boring. On the other hand, Greens can be seen as impatient and critical.

A Green mated to a Green could be a union lacking in warmth, passion, and sizzling sex. Life could be so structured as to be boring. Even the arguments could be carefully organized rationalizations directed at solving the surface problem without addressing the inner issues.

A Green is often uninterested in rationalizing emotions, which is basic to a Nurturing Tan's mental process. Greens can be the users in this relationship, more interested in what Nurturing Tans can do for them than in what they can contribute to the relationship. A Nurturing Tan is all too willing to do all the work after the Green has posed a solution to the problem—theoretically, at least.

Greens and Loving Tans are like oil and water. Their thought processes are the antithesis of one another: Greens are so analytical and Loving Tans so random. The cloud of confusion that constantly surrounds a Loving Tan will drive a Green to distraction. Impatience, frustration, and exasperation mark a relationship between a Green and a Loving Tan.

Emotional/Spiritual Colors

Blues possess too many uncataloged emotions to be comfortable mates for Greens. While the Green appreciates the love and nurturing available from a Blue, the lack of organizational thinking is difficult for a Green to handle.

Green and Violet can be a dynamic team, especially if they see that their goal or mission in life is to practice what they preach, to be living examples of their beliefs. Greens follow the one-year plan and Violets follow the five-year plan; with the short-term and the long-term views covered, they have a system that is guaranteed not to fail. However, Violets who are unwilling to share their deepest thoughts with their Green mates are in for trouble.

Greens and Lavenders think alike. Greens see a pattern through time; Lavenders see a pattern through space. Therefore, they have many areas where their minds can meet. It is as if the Lavenders provide the raw material of ideas and images and Greens put them together into a comprehensive whole. There is a great deal of elemental excitement available in this sort of collaboration.

Greens are the one Personality Spectrums color that Crystals can tolerate without being fractured by the energy. Within a Green's auric field, a Crystal is able to maintain his or her emotional equilibrium and be a contributing partner.

Greens intellectually appreciate the learning style of the Indigos and are willing to give them the latitude to be who they need to be. However, Greens find it difficult to handle the Indigos' insistence on doing things their way over a long period of time, especially if the Indigos ignore the Greens' needs.

PERSONAL POWER AND LEADERSHIP STYLE

Greens lead by giving information and ideas. They do not administer with personal power or charisma. They are loners needing autonomy and personal space. However aloof and self-assured Greens seem to be, they thrive on recognition. Their satisfaction comes from providing the good ideas, and they want to be acknowledged as the source of those ideas. Greens lead by demonstrating their willingness to think ideas through instead of getting caught up in the emotional fervor of the moment.

Greens are astute in the ways of business; they are articulate, insightful, and generous with their ideas. Greens prefer being powerful in settings where their ideas can be quickly implemented. They enjoy pulling the strings behind the scenes as well as accepting the applause on stage. With the insights provided by a Green—especially in marketing, public relations, advertising, and finance—many businesses can thrive and prosper. The leadership skills of Greens allow them to be excellent consultants, therapists, organizers, and planners.

FINANCIAL CHOICES

Because Greens know how to be productive and creative, they are wise with finances and natural moneymakers. They comprehend the ideas behind money and they intuitively understand the nature of the financial system. Greens regard finances as a game, a challenge, and sometimes will make and lose large sums over and over. When the rest of the population is digging out from under a crash in the market, a Green will have figured a way to profit from it.

Greens tend to be attracted to professions where ideas and money come together—venture capital, investments, stock brokerage, writing, and publishing.

Greens do not like to have a ceiling on their income potential. They prefer occupations that offer unlimited financial opportunity such as sales, where the incentives are greater. They prefer selling high-ticket items such as real estate, cars, furs, jewelry, and insurance, because a Green knows how to take advantage of the bonus and incentive opportunities available.

Greens love money and all the things it can buy—luxury, convenience, quality, and beauty. The Greens' love of order and symmetry allows them to appreciate fine workmanship and quality materials. Though Greens are not extravagant, they will not settle for less than what they want. A Green will do without rather than accept poor workmanship or a model they don't like.

Greens are meticulous recordkeepers who pay close attention to their finances. Their personal and business records are current; accounts are paid as soon as the bills arrive, and checkbooks are balanced against bank statements.

CAREER OPTIONS

Because Greens are so productive, creative, and skillful at planning, organizing, and mapping out campaign strategy, they do well in advertising, marketing, and public relations. They also make good campaign managers, party planners, and special events coordinators.

Greens also do well in occupations that revolve around money—the larger the amounts, the better. Therefore, they do well in sales, financial planning, insurance, stocks and bonds, and commodities.

And finally, because Greens see patterns so clearly, they make excellent therapists, diagnosticians, analysts, and counselors.

SPIRITUALITY

To Greens, spirituality is an idea. If they give an idea sufficient time and study, they can assimilate it. Hence, Greens tend to approach spirituality as a mental challenge, a particularly interesting puzzle. Greens want to reason their way to spiritual understanding, often omitting the emotional component that, to others, is an integral part of spirituality.

The Higher Power, to a Green, is the *mind* behind the creation of this reality. The spiritual search for a Green is an attempt to conceptualize the mind of God. Greens hold the concept of a Creator as the perfect idea. In comparing the lack of perfection in themselves to the perfection of this Higher Power, Greens become mired in despair and frustration, resulting in a slow descent into depression. Because the task of knowing God seems so overwhelming, Greens may see it as a challenge to their own self-worth. The spiritual opportunity for Greens is to accept themselves, knowing that their contribution is good enough. Part of learning to understand themselves is to come to terms with the concept of grace, to know that they are entitled to universal love without having to earn it or deserve it. For Greens, spirituality is the development of the trust to release the project once they have done all they can and believe the universe will balance the difference.

Greens will actively seek spirituality as they enter young adulthood. This quest will lead them to explore many different philosophies and beliefs. They are seeking the one key—knowledge, meditation, activism, chanting, ritual—that will open the door to an understanding of the divine in themselves.

TEN

NURTURING TAN

Nurturing Tans are another of the Eclipse Colors in the Personality Spectrums system. The color closest to their body is Mental Tan. Outside the Mental Tan and completely encircling their body is a band of Blue. These two colors combine many of the characteristics of both the Mental Family of colors and the Emotional/Spiritual Family of colors. However, a Nurturing Tan has a distinctly different motivation from either of these two colors alone, with personality and character traits unique to this color.

The driving force of the Nurturing Tans, the mission that gives their lives meaning, is the concept of brotherhood. They demonstrate their commitment to this mission by rendering service to the family, the neighborhood, the city, the nation, or the world. They put the needs of others before their own, teaching humanitarianism by example.

The lesson that Nurturing Tans need to learn is to identify and serve their own personal ego needs as well and to satisfy their own longings and desires in such a way as to make existence something worth living for. Nurturing Tans need to learn that it is acceptable to give something to themselves while serving others.

APPROACH TO PHYSICAL REALITY

Tenacious, determined, dedicated—these are the words that most accurately describe a Nurturing Tan's attitude to-

124

ward the physical. Given any project that requires action, Nurturing Tans approach it with perseverance and dogged determination. When faced with a deadline, they are single-minded in their effort to achieve completion.

When working on projects, Nurturing Tans gather together all the materials and supplies necessary, then lay out the parts of the project to be worked on. If one section is lagging or needs more work at this phase, they feel more comfortable working on that part first. When all parts are ready, they start at the beginning and plow through the whole project from beginning to end. They are reluctant to take breaks for fear of losing momentum and not completing the project within the time they have given themselves.

Nurturing Tans, like all the Mental Family colors, tend to approach the physical aspects of life through reason and mental processes. They must think about the physicality of a thing first. Once they are able to interact with it, they create an organizational system that embraces both the physical and theoretical, and thereby make the overall concept work.

Nowhere is this process more evident than in the way Nurturing Tans approach physical health and well-being. They attempt to understand the mechanics of their body, the purpose of each diet and fitness recommendation, before they begin the regimen.

MENTAL ATTITUDES

The thinking process of the Nurturing Tan, as with all the Mental Personality Spectrums colors, is logical, sequential, and orderly: 1, 2, 3, 4, 5, 6, 7, 8, 9, 10. However, for a Nurturing Tan, intervening steps 3, 6, and 9 must be directed toward the emotions of the individuals involved in the decision-making process. The Nurturing Tans' gift is their willingness to take others' feelings into consideration even though feelings cannot be translated into something tangible.

For Nurturing Tans, communication is crucial. In problem-solving, step 1 is the definition of the problem. Step 2 is collecting data and formulating tentative solutions. Step 3 is finding out how everybody feels about the process so far. Only

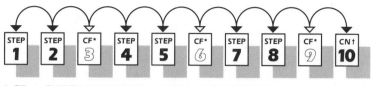

* CF = CHECK FEELINGS   †CN = CONSENSUS

when all concerned individuals have had an opportunity to express how they feel will a Nurturing Tan move forward to a redefinition of the problem based on all the information collected to that point. The Nurturing Tans' mental process may seem slow and cumbersome to individuals who want instant answers and solutions, but when an organization is ready to move forward, everyone is committed to the Nurturing Tans' plan of action because it was achieved by consensus.

Nurturing Tans' skill lies in their ability to listen to the deep, unspoken needs of others. They are able to track the emotional tone of a group while simultaneously following the flow of information from its members. Nurturing Tans have the ability to put into words what others feel, without passing judgment. They combine the compassion of the Blue with the intellectual acumen of the Mental Tan.

This Personality Spectrums color knows and understands that human emotion is a necessary and important part of the data required to make decisions to which others can commit themselves emotionally as well as mentally. Intuitively, they know that without emotional commitment, camaraderie, and enhanced self-esteem, no project or outcome is truly satisfying; it is merely a demonstration of form without substance.

Nurturing Tans are meticulous in their thought processes. This attribute carries over into everything they do and they check for errors and omissions at every step along the way. To others, this can seem very laborious and time-consuming. It must be remembered, however, that Nurturing Tans are aware of both left-brain information and right-brain emotion; therefore, they have a great need for mental order. At home and at work, they create systems so that they can move easily from one project to another, keeping tabs on all of the details.

Without these systems, a Nurturing Tan can become bogged down in boring, time-consuming details.

EMOTIONAL MAKEUP

Nurturing Tans are happiest when working with a group of people. Because they consider the impact of every decision on the people involved, they lack the dynamic drive it takes to be aggressive, bottom-line businesspersons. Nurturing Tans know how to listen with their hearts as well as their minds; therefore, their problem-solving strategies are win-win solutions for client/customer, employee/supervisor, husband/wife. Nurturing Tans are concerned not only with where they are going but also with how they should get there. In business dealings, they are patient, intent on understanding others' points of view and thinking patterns. They seldom leap to conclusions or resort to stereotypes.

Nurturing Tans are compassionate and loving. They are the most unselfish of all the Personality Spectrums colors. They are able to be nurturing and supportive without demanding allegiance or payment in return. Shy and self-effacing, they are unwilling to attract undue attention to themselves. In their eagerness to serve others, they tend to put everyone else's needs ahead of their own. Problems may arise when their unselfish gestures are taken for granted by others. This behavior deprives Nurturing Tans of the recognition that their ego needs and that their selflessness deserves.

The problem for Nurturing Tans is that they seldom give thought to personal gratification or self-importance. Nurturing Tans must learn to give time and thought to what makes them happy, fulfilled, and satisfied. They must then communicate those requirements to others. Because Nurturing Tans are so self-effacing, others may assume that they don't need or want anything in return for their efforts. That is not the case. And unless they have another Nurturing Tan in their life, chances are that no one will take the time or have the patience to listen as attentively to the Nurturing Tans as they are willing to listen to others.

Nurturing Tans cheerfully give to others simply because

they have something to give. They give because they have a deep love, compassion, and understanding of human nature. The continuity of their relationships gives them a sense of identity, a way of situating themselves in time and space. Nurturing Tans know who they are by the people they have in their lives. This Personality Spectrums color knows the meaning of the old adage, ''Tell me who your friends are and I'll tell you who you are.'' Their concept of community can be as small as their immediate family or as large as the whole world.

Whatever their general frame of reference, the Nurturing Tans' most important social unit is the family. Nurturing Tans usually mate for life. Loving, nurturing, and caring for the family gives them peace and satisfaction. As parents, they are active and involved, often participating in their children's activities, spending quality time with them, taking a genuine interest in what they are thinking and doing. Men who are Nurturing Tans tend to get more actively involved with their children's activities by becoming scout masters, coaches, or group leaders. They are firm and logical in their discipline, always willing to listen to the child's story while remaining firmly in the adult role.

Family gatherings, outings, and vacations are important activities to Nurturing Tan parents. They realize that certain kinds of communication need the seclusion of a family on vacation, far from the hustle and bustle of everyday life. Because much of a Nurturing Tan's emotional renewal is provided within the nuclear family, a loving, supportive, emotionally secure family life is a necessity.

As the natural listeners of the Personality Spectrums, Nurturing Tans have the ability to identify the crux of an issue from the ''story'' or the nonessential data. They listen with their minds and hearts, truly hearing the hopes, fears, and longings buried deep inside the individual who is speaking. Their gift is to be able to listen actively, assisting others in organizing their options and selecting a plan of action. However, a Nurturing Tan needs to benefit from this type of communicating as much as others do. There is no gift so precious to Nurturing Tans as to be heard with understanding and compassion by those they love. Unfortunately, because they are so good at listening themselves, Nurturing Tans seldom experience the same in return. And because of their unassuming natures, they will not ask for what their souls hunger for—understanding and compassion.

SOCIAL STYLE

Nurturing Tans are community minded and community oriented, always seeing issues from the perspective of the impact on the people involved, whether family, neighborhood, city, or world. They are also able to see the concept behind the issue, the larger picture, the greater context. They become involved in many different grass-roots projects whose goals are to improve the quality of human life.

Nurturing Tans love people and love to be a part of a group, usually putting down deep emotional roots. They have many friends, but they form bonds of intimacy slowly over a long period of time. They interact at a warm, human level, supporting and enabling others. They are always willing to lend a hand by participating in those activities they believe in. They prefer the role of participant-observer so that they can be actively involved while maintaining a watchful objective distance. They never push themselves on others, and are unwilling to impose their ideas, attitudes, or beliefs where they are not wanted or have not been invited.

This Personality Spectrums color is social and sociable. People love being around Nurturing Tans because they enhance the mood of celebration in social occasions.

COMPATIBILITY

Physical (environmental) Colors

The Physical (environmental) Colors seem to be too bold and brash to form compatible relationships with Nurturing Tans.

The fun-loving rowdiness of a Red adds life and sparkle to any party, but Reds are too forceful for a Nurturing Tan to be comfortable with over a long period of time.

Oranges' love of excitement and thrills keeps Nurturing Tans on the brink of a nervous breakdown, making them feel emotionally vulnerable and unsafe.

Magentas, with their need to be free and uncommitted, find the Nurturing Tans' need to be committed stultifying and inhibiting.

Physical (body) Colors

The playful aspects of the Yellow bring out the protective, loving, nurturing qualities in the Nurturing Tan. A Yellow's love of life lightens the Nurturing Tan's tendency to be serious and purposeful.

The silent, introspective nature of the Physical Tan causes alarm buttons to go off within a Nurturing Tan's head. Whenever Nurturing Tans perceive that someone is withdrawing from them, they immediately jump to the conclusion that they have done something wrong. Therefore in a relationship between a Nurturing Tan and a Physical Tan, emotional insecurity runs rife.

Mental Colors

Mental Tans and Nurturing Tans seem to be on the same intellectual wavelength. Both are cautious and careful in their opinions and behaviors. They seem to understand each other, lending support and information. This is not a relationship accompanied by spectacular emotional fireworks. Instead, a steady, quiet calm pervades. Some people perceive this as boredom.

Some Greens and Nurturing Tans are like oil and water, but others mix quite well. This depends on how soon a decision needs to be made. If the Green has plenty of lead time, then he or she can accept and appreciate the methodical process of the Nurturing Tan. However, if a rapid decision is necessary, a Green can become impatient and caustic. The Nurturing Tan is also more interested in emotions than in outcomes, and this tendency conflicts with a Green's natural style.

Nurturing Tans who marry Nurturing Tans are like brother and sister. The relationship is deeply loving, but not sexually exciting. There is a high degree of cooperation, intuitive understanding, and commitment when both partners are Nurturing Tans.

The way of life of the Loving Tan is too haphazard and confusing for a Nurturing Tan. The Nurturing Tan's protective instincts grow so strong that he or she becomes the surrogate parent of the Loving Tan. This can create resentment and diminish the self-worth and self-respect of both parties.

Emotional/Spiritual Colors

Blues are able to keep the sexual and emotional fires stoked while at the same time allowing the Nurturing Tan to create a calm, serene home environment. Neither Blues nor Nurturing Tans like confrontation; fights and harsh words are seldom heard.

Violets have strong personalities coupled with emotional and intuitive capabilities that provide the ideal counterbalance to the gentleness of the Nurturing Tan. The Violet's need to be the visionary combines very well with the Nurturing Tan's need to support a larger vision. The Violet, however, must learn to share the credit while the Nurturing Tan must learn to demand his or her due.

Lavenders do not provide enough ballast for a successful relationship with a Nurturing Tan. When faced with the vicissitudes of life, a Lavender escapes, leaving the Nurturing Tan to cope alone. A Nurturing Tan wants and needs a partner, but a Lavender is not available emotionally.

Crystals and Indigos are too remote, emotionally, to make good partners for Nurturing Tans. A Nurturing Tan's need to pay attention to details can cause anxiety and uneasiness in a Crystal, too. Indigo's ability to simply *be* is in direct opposition to a Nurturing Tan's need for constant interaction with ideas and things.

PERSONAL POWER AND LEADERSHIP STYLE

Nurturing Tans' strength lies in their ability to bring together a group of people diversified in outlook and form them into a coordinated team. As ''people persons,'' Nurturing Tans know the value of the adage, "You can catch more flies with honey than you can with vinegar." They gain cooperation and support by considering the emotional needs of everyone involved in the project—team members, contractors, suppliers, customers, and employer. Another strength is their willingness to work behind the scenes, executing contracts and agreements that are consistent with the stated needs of those involved.

Nurturing Tans often will take on leadership tasks others decline as being too controversial or not glamorous enough, such as affirmative action in the workplace or planning the company picnic. Nurturing Tans quietly go about making a difference. They care deeply about human rights issues. They settle the squabbles among siblings with the same equanimity that they bring to bear on corporate politics. As leaders, they give of their time, talent, and energy to make positive humanitarian changes within their sphere of influence.

In the world of business and commerce, Nurturing Tans combine their interest in social welfare with economic innovations such as intrapreneurship, a system whereby employees sell their ideas and inventions to the parent company in exchange for the opportunity to manage the division responsible for manufacturing or developing that idea or product. Employee-owned companies, like Air West, also appeal to Nurturing Tans.

In whatever field or occupation they find themselves, the main role of Nurturing Tans is to assist groups of people to interact with one another with compassion and caring. They love teaching others, and they demonstrate infinite patience in helping each person in the group grasp each concept. Nurturing Tans do well wherever clear communication is essential to the process. As such, they make excellent division or team managers.

FINANCIAL CHOICES

Nurturing Tans have a kind of faith about money and how their financial needs will be met. They know they will always somehow be provided for; therefore, they go about their business with confidence. This is not to imply that Nurturing Tans are not aware of the value and power of money. Nurturing Tans, in fact, husband their resources and are prudent without being overly cautious, shrewd without being parsimonious. They are wise, deft, and generous. They give to individuals and to organizations that maintain human dignity and promote self-worth and self-esteem.

Nurturing Tans are good providers for their families, conscious of their loved ones' need for security. They choose investments that are safe. They judge the amount they must earn by the needs of their family and community. They tend to invest in their own homes and businesses. They are not conspicuous consumers, but tend to purchase products that are well-engineered and durable rather than those that reflect passing fashions or fads. They most often purchase unpretentious but comfortable homes and dependable, well-engineered automobiles of which they can be proud for years.

Nurturing Tans perceive that children are the most essential resource of any community and that well-educated children have a greater chance of becoming productive members of society. Nurturing Tans support various community activities that enrich human life: theater, opera, symphony, children's sport leagues. They often assume leadership positions on boards of recreation or education.

CAREER OPTIONS

Because of their listening skills, Nurturing Tans make excellent arbitrators, judges, counselors, personnel directors, trainers, and teachers. Their choice of occupations often mirrors their love of people and their willingness to be of help. One way this Personality Spectrums color serves is by bringing calm reasonableness to bear on emotionally charged situations, assisting people to communicate better with one another.

In the workplace, if a Nurturing Tan has difficulty with an individual in authority, then the authority figure is a genuinely difficult person to work with. Nurturing Tans can get along with virtually everyone. On the job, they have the ability to be compliant without being obsequious.

Nurturing Tans are serious, reflective individuals. They are never self-seeking in their service, and therefore do not generally choose high-profile careers as professional athletes or nightclub entertainers. However, in response to their social conscience, they will run for public office, accepting a public-service post for the purpose of giving voice to their ideals. Out of their love for community, they often work to better it, creating a model for their view of the world. In order to make their dream of a better world real, they become real-estate agents, developers, planners. They love creating environments that enhance and enlarge the capacity for positive human interaction.

Nurturing Tans do not do well working alone or in competition with others. Careers as writers, artists, or designers would require them to spend too many long hours alone. To work only with machinery or equipment, as computer programmers or technicians do, would make a Nurturing Tan feel cut off from human interaction. Any job that puts Nurturing Tans in deliberate opposition to or in physical combat with others, such as the military, professional boxing, or police work, goes against the natural grain of their peacemaking gifts and talents.

They do well in occupations that combine the use of delicate, complicated machinery with human interaction skills: dentistry, optometry, radiology, medicine. While they love what computers can do, Nurturing Tans find that computer technology, in and of itself, is too boring, linear, and devoid of human emotion to be a satisfactory way to make a living.

SPIRITUALITY

Nurturing Tans are most interested in theologies and religions that stress the human element: compassion, love, and the inherent goodness of mankind. They are suspicious of any philosophy or theology that has no practical application. Nurturing Tans easily put into practice what they learn in church.

For them, lofty ideals are the touchstones of reality. "Love one another" is the plan of action for a Nurturing Tan.

This Personality Spectrums color serves God by serving humankind. The Good Samaritan must have been a Nurturing Tan; he interrupted his journey to take his injured enemy to the nearest inn, bind up his wounds, and pay for his lodging without thought of what he would get in return. Nurturing Tans feel compelled to put into practice the principles they have learned, wedding deep spiritual compassion to their practical everyday activities. Nurturing Tans live to know God, often experiencing this knowing through the eyes of those they love and serve. To be separated from other people who need their gift of service is, for a Nurturing Tan, to be bereft of God.

This color counsels with compassion, serves with dignity. Nurturing Tans most often choose to be involved with the social welfare services provided by churches—rescue missions, community outreach programs, and children's day care and preschool programs. Nurturing Tans serve because of their intense commitment to issues of human dignity and community involvement, and not for the recognition, status, or benefits associated with the organization.

With their intense commitment to the community and the individuals who compose it, Nurturing Tans are the spiritual midwives in this time of burgeoning spirituality. Nurturing Tans' spiritual quest is to demonstrate how to create resolution within ourselves. This heightened sense of personal peace, dignity, self-worth, and self-esteem will assist us in developing a sense of world fellowship.

ELEVEN

LOVING TAN

Loving Tan is another Personality Spectrums color that is distinguished by an eclipse, a second band of color, which is Red. The Red surrounds the inner basic color, Mental Tan. The Red Eclipse adds the component of unconditional love.

Loving Tans are bright and inquisitive, and have a love of people. However, theirs is an abstract love of humanity rather than a love of specific human beings. Because of their ability to stand apart and observe the human condition without passing judgment, Loving Tans are uniquely equipped to serve as the bridge of communication as our world shifts focus and priorities. Loving Tans are able to see the shifting patterns in all areas of human endeavor—law, education, government, economics, and world trade. They are able to distinguish those patterns that are emerging from those that are ebbing. Because this is a natural perceptive talent of Loving Tans, they are able to use it objectively.

Loving Tans tend to be the objective observers of life, unlike the Nurturing Tans who tend to be the participant-observers. The challenge for Loving Tans is to learn to focus and direct their energies and abilities rather than scattering them in all directions. Loving Tans are able to see all the separate pieces at once; at the same time they can appreciate the overall pattern of a puzzle. When they become fragmented, they are overwhelmed and confused, and distrust their own inner process.

136

APPROACH TO PHYSICAL REALITY

Loving Tans have an affinity to nature and the outdoors. The environment fulfills for them a tactile need that working in the realm of ideas does not. Loving Tans also experience nature to be the one constant in their lives, the one thing they can count on in a world continually shifting and changing. They love to spend time gardening, feeling their hands in the soil—a sensation that reminds them of the timelessness of the cycles of nature. This activity also has its own self-imposed order, since there can be no harvest before the seed is planted. Ordinarily the Loving Tan wants to leap ahead of the step-by-step process and work on all aspects simultaneously. But nature has its own internal integrity. The mental discipline that is fostered by the physical activity of gardening assists Loving Tans in curtailing the flightiness of their thought process.

Because Loving Tans are members of the Mental Family of Personality Spectrums colors, being outdoors is not inherent to their nature and gives them a new perspective on life. Loving Tans can get bogged down in activities that are primarily intellectual, cutting themselves off from other people. Physical exertions such as bicycling, walking, or swimming get them out of their heads and into the world of people. Because they are so open and friendly, Loving Tans never lack for companionship in their exercise activities.

Loving Tans are not attached to possessions such as furniture or the other trappings of life. (However, they do love mechanical gadgets and electronic toys, as do all of the Mental Family colors.) Possessions are seen only as the means of achieving goals or outcomes, not as the objective.

MENTAL ATTITUDES

While Loving Tans are one of the Mental Family colors, their thinking process is different from the logical, linear model of the other Mental colors. Loving Tans think in a matrix or a mind map. In other words, they make their mental connections randomly. Instead of the neat, orderly one-two-three process of the Mental Tans, the Loving Tans' process is random. They see the last step as just one component of a set needed to reach the goal, not as the final step of a process. Because they see all of the steps simultaneously, they have great difficulty deciding which one to take first—in other words, they experience difficulty organizing their priorities, either by degree of importance or by time limitations.

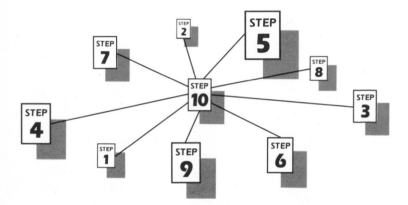

The mind of a Loving Tan is similar to a butterfly net; it is useful for catching interesting ideas. Loving Tans live in a place in their minds that has no time. To a Loving Tan, pieces of information are like the bits of colored glass in the kaleidoscope of life—continuously moving, constantly changing, never settling into a stationary pattern.

Like Physical Tans, Loving Tans feel inadequate because their mental process is so different from everyone else's. As children, they are ignored, made fun of, or not taken seriously. Their ideas are often discounted because parents and siblings are unable to see the pattern of their thoughts, the big picture in which details show up as individual projects. Part of the problem is that Loving Tans work on all aspects of a project simultaneously, a process as difficult for others to follow as it is for a Loving Tan to explain.

Loving Tans experience time as circular. They have little relationship to or understanding of the concepts of past, present, and future. When describing events in their lives, they can recall events of twenty years ago with the same clarity as they remember what happened just last week. As Loving Tans relate their stories, the listener must remember to ask for time clues; otherwise, the sequence of events will not be clear.

This lack of a linear sense of time causes Loving Tans frustration in dealing with the details of their lives. It also has repercussions in their careers or business dealings, giving them a reputation for being undependable and unreliable. They are not able to make rational step-by-step decisions regarding the best utilization of their time or talents. Every option receives equal consideration, and the project of the moment has the highest priority. Loving Tans frequently are unable to honor their commitments to others because they get involved in something else on the way, losing track of time and previous obligations.

For Loving Tans, organizing their time, destinations, and commitments logically or sequentially is very difficult. They are chronically late, showing up in the right place on the wrong date and vice versa, and overscheduling their time. They also have difficulty deciding what to do with things that do not fall into easily identifiable categories. Clothing goes into closets, of course; socks, underwear, scarves, and jewelry go into the dresser drawers. But with paperwork, where the distinctions are not so clear-cut, organization becomes a mystery to the Loving Tan. Categories, headings, and titles overlap one another in a confusing array of options and systems. Loving Tans will hunt for a lost document randomly in a search that is neither logical nor sequential. Instead of going through the file cabinets drawer by drawer and file by file, they will skip around, looking under every category they can think of, often duplicating their efforts, and compounding their anger at themselves and their ways.

Because Loving Tans' mental process is so random, they learn best by immersing themselves in a subject that interests them. They learn a foreign language, for example, by going to the country where it is spoken, and they go there alone, so that they have no choice but to learn. Like the Indigo children, Loving Tans do not function well in the current educational system where one studies math for one hour first thing every morning, followed by literature for the second hour, and so forth throughout the day. In fact, this system causes physical pain for Loving Tans, because they are jerked from one mind-set, or frame of reference, to another every hour. Just when they get interested in a book or a laboratory experiment, it is time for lunch or history.

When Loving Tans are fascinated by a subject, or when they need it for economic or physical survival, they learn quickly, absorb vast amounts of information, and often become experts in fields in which they have no formal training. Their random sorting process allows them to read huge quantities of material, sifting and sorting out only the most relevant issues within that discipline.

EMOTIONAL MAKEUP

The Red Eclipse of the Loving Tan adds the aura of childlike eagerness to the staid profundity of a Mental Tan. Eagerness, willingness, and optimism characterize their interactions with life, people, and ideas.

Loving Tans, despite their Red Eclipse, do not have the dynamic, forward-thrusting energy of a Red overlay. Instead, the eclipse gives them a childlike eagerness to please, a need to be accepted, protected, and loved. Like Blues and Nurturing Tans, Loving Tans need a mate who is emotionally stronger than they are, psychologically grounded, and physically able to cope with the exigencies of daily life. Because Loving Tans live in their heads, which are usually in the clouds, they need stabilizing forces, individuals and situations to assist them in establishing priorities and setting goals.

In order to protect themselves from being hurt, Loving Tans tend to discuss feelings, attitudes, and beliefs—all highly charged components of any relationship—from the lofty realm of abstraction. The question most often asked of Loving Tans is "What does all that theory mean for me, in my life?" This often launches the Loving Tans onto another tangent as obtuse as the original, demonstrating their inability to choose the appropriate thought or idea and apply it to the present situation.

Loving and trusting as children, they are tolerated but not understood. Too often they are brushed off by the adults in their lives who are unable to comprehend their gentle, abstract natures and are unwilling to listen to their lofty ideas. Loving Tans are frequently taken for granted and become less and less willing to share the deeper parts of themselves as they become older and more wary. Ultimately, they often become emotionally disengaged from the deep, feeling side of their personalities, substituting the inconsequential for the essential.

Emotionally, Loving Tans have the capacity to love and care about a great many people in an abstract sort of way. However, they seem to be unable to develop truly intimate relationships because they don't trust others. Their childlike openness and eagerness inspire them to give freely of their time, talent, and possessions. However, too often their generosity is misunderstood and unappreciated. While they maintain their broad, overall faith in the goodness of humanity, Loving Tans become very cautious about committing themselves to specific individuals or situations. This causes them to become increasingly aloof in all their relationships, and their detachment often culminates in loneliness, helplessness, and an inability to know how or where to reconnect emotionally.

Loving Tans look to marriage and family for understanding, love, and intimacy. They often have an adolescent picture of what marriage or partnering will require of them and what they require from the relationship. They can see the potential in the relationship; they simply do not know how to balance and fulfill the requirements of intimacy, love, responsibility, and nurturing. Often, Loving Tans use marriage or a relationship as their touchstone, or emotional security blanket, relying on their partners to provide the financial and emotional stability in the relationship.

Because Loving Tans are mentally and often emotionally unavailable, their partners tend to become demanding and to treat them as overgrown children. This puts a limit on the intimacy that they can experience within the relationship. Loving Tans feel jerked into an adult reality that they feel unequipped to cope with; the partner, in turn, feels unappreciated, unacknowledged, and unsupported.

If Loving Tans have several relationships in which they do not experience the deep level of love and acceptance they want and need, they often withdraw emotionally and settle into a relationship of convenience, or they fall in love with someone who is moving to Tahiti in three months. The ensuing pattern of loneliness is a haunting ache deep within them, which they camouflage with their warm, outgoing personalities.

SOCIAL STYLE

Loving Tans tend to be among the "social" Personality Spectrums colors, enjoying get-togethers, parties, dinners— any occasion at which people meet and mingle. However, because of their random thinking process, Loving Tans have difficulty setting priorities on their social calendar, and they may schedule too many activities on a single day. Then, in order to please everyone, they rush from activity to activity, event to event, not really making contact with any one group of people.

Loving Tans love exchanging ideas and concepts with a number of people. They pay attention to those with whom they are interacting, and they learn some tidbit of obscure information from every encounter. However, Loving Tans are unable to sustain the emotional exchange because after the transfer of information they do not know how to move the conversation, or the relationship, to a deeper personal level of sharing. True intimacy is difficult for Loving Tans to achieve.

Loving Tans are fascinated by other cultures and other ethnic groups, and exhibit a broad-minded tolerance and respect for the different ways people do things. In their innocent inquisitiveness, they have many experiences not usually afforded the average traveler. Loving Tans lovingly respect differences between cultures and groups, and are willing to laugh at themselves as they learn the language and social customs of another country.

COMPATIBILITY WITH OTHER COLORS

Physical (environmental) Colors

Reds have the grounded, solid, pragmatic energy that Loving Tans need to be able to function effectively and effi-

ciently in the world. Loving Tans give the Reds the unconditional love they need. In this marriage or partnership each
mate supplies what the other is missing.

Oranges' way of thinking and living is the very antithesis
of Loving Tans'. Oranges are independent, not needing
anyone for anything, whereas Loving Tans need someone to
be in their corner, someone with whom they can interact and
relate. Oranges do not want to be responsible for anyone, and
a Loving Tan can be seen as a responsibility.

Magentas find the random thought process of a Loving
Tan too difficult to cope with on a day-to-day basis. Magentas
are nonconformists, but that does not mean that they are space
cadets or weirdos. They do not see themselves as caretakers,
and there is a part of every Loving Tan that needs to be taken
care of.

Physical (body) Colors

Yellows are active, vital, and enthusiastic participants in
life. Loving Tans are attracted to this childlike playfulness, but
they find it difficult to be in a relationship with a Yellow who
refuses to settle down and get serious.

Because Physical Tans and Loving Tans both deal with
their feelings in an abstract manner, they will not be comfortable together for a long period of time. Physical Tans do not
know how to extrapolate their feelings, and Loving Tans want
to extrapolate them into the largest possible context. This
proclivity for abstraction of the Loving Tan is difficult for a
Physical Tan, a concrete thinker, to relate to.

Mental Colors

Mental Tans and Loving Tans form friendships that are
lasting and deep because they speak the same intellectual
language. However, in love relationships, they can both fail to
address the emotional issues—Mental Tans because they want
to think the problem through to solution, and Loving Tans
because they see the problem not as one that hinders the
individual relationship but rather as one that holds back man-

kind. That kind of abstract thinking is very hard on a relationship.

Greens are rational, capable of leaping to answers and conclusions based on very little information or data. Loving Tans' random thinking, as a result, scrambles all of the Greens' mental channels. Greens assume that as the information emerges from a Loving Tan, it is in order when, in fact, it is not. Therefore, Greens leap to conclusions that are not even in the realm of possibilities for a Loving Tan.

Nurturing Tans listen with an open and nonjudgmental heart to the multiplicity of plans and ideas that exist in a Loving Tan's mind. The Nurturing Tan is able to sift and sort through the information and details in order to find those that will make a plan or idea work. Nurturing Tans are willing to assist by creating the organizational systems that help keep a Loving Tan on target.

Loving Tans mated to Loving Tans will make people wonder who is minding the store. With both partners living in their heads, making random connections of information, and leaving personal possessions everywhere, little is accomplished. It is not that the partners are inept or stupid, but that they both have their own list of priorities which, in typical Loving Tan fashion, they have failed to share with their partner.

Emotional/Spiritual Colors

Blues serve as a steadying influence for the Loving Tan, sensing their deep need for understanding and patience. The Blues receive the unconditional love they require in return for the nurturing they give.

Violets are a strong balance in the life of a Loving Tan. With their didactic and dictatorial manner and their capacity to see beyond the mundane, Violets help the Loving Tan sift and sort through their projects, choosing those that will have the most beneficial impact on society. The Loving Tans bring balance to the relationship with a Violet.

Lavenders and Loving Tans have emotional processes that are antagonistic to each other; this precludes a truly successful marriage or partnership. Both partners back away from intimacy for fear of being consumed by the needs of the other and of the relationship. Both attempt to cling to their autonomy at the expense of the relationship.

Crystals have a difficult time dealing with the natural scatteredness of the Loving Tan, which causes the Crystal confusion and agitation. When they are with Loving Tans, Crystals may find themselves feeling anxious and upset and acting fretful and demanding, without even knowing why.

Indigos and Loving Tans have a natural affinity for one another. They have similar ways of viewing the world, although their motivations are different. The Loving Tan gives the Indigo a great deal of emotional, intellectual, and physical freedom, and the Indigo responds with trust and love. These two Personality Spectrums colors are the most difficult for others to understand, but to each other, they are an open book.

PERSONAL POWER AND LEADERSHIP STYLE

Loving Tans do not exhibit natural leadership abilities. They are more apt to lead by virtue of their love and appreciation of other people. They lack the dynamic forcefulness and farsightedness of a Violet. As head of a committee, a Loving Tan will have too many people doing too many different things. This aura lacks the ability to grasp a project firmly and may be unable to delegate responsibility effectively. When a Loving Tan is in charge, no one seems to know where a project is in its development until the last minute—when it all seems to come together, miraculously, in typical Loving Tan fashion.

Loving Tans work best in one-on-one situations, guiding, directing, and teaching with infinite patience. They love to give to others what they have most needed and wanted themselves—an opportunity to work on all facets of a project simultaneously. Therefore, their skill is in mentoring and tutoring, not in a highly structured group situation. They excel when allowed to work at their occupation while acting as mentors. Given a student who is interested in their field, Loving Tans will generously share their vast store of information and experience. Because Loving Tans are generally self-taught and curious, they are usually experts in several unrelated fields of interest. Their inquisitiveness, coupled with their need to understand each idea from several points of view, makes Loving Tans especially good with Indigo children. Loving Tans modify their random thought process with patience and a willingness to spend the time necessary to make sure that the Indigo child truly understands a concept. In addition, Loving Tans gently and lovingly accept the differentness of an Indigo and remain unperturbed by the apparent remoteness exhibited by an Indigo. Loving Tans do not need to have emotional allegiance in order to be effective mentors. Since Indigos form only a few deep emotional attachments, this relationship works well for both.

FINANCIAL CHOICES

Unlike all the other colors in the Mental Family, Loving Tans do not regard finance as a simple exercise in mathematics, a listing of assets and liabilities. The whole concept of money and budgets is a major challenge for them. Because budgets are made up of numbers, which are, by nature, logical and sequential, they present a special challenge to a Loving Tan whose process is neither logical nor sequential. Loving Tans have the capacity to calculate what it will take for them to manage their own individual economic needs and wants. However, when they attempt to expand the formula to include the needs and wants of others, such as mates and children, or to take into consideration emergencies or contingencies, they are unable to make a budget work.

In an attempt to be responsible and to keep logical records of their income and their expenditures, Loving Tans often buy an elaborate record book and record in it their expenses and income. However, they tend to get bogged down in the intricacies of the bookkeeping system instead of evaluating how well it works—as if the system itself will solve their budgeting problems.

Because Loving Tans have difficulty keeping track of their money, they also have difficulty hanging on to their possessions. Loving Tans often have so many ideas, schedules, and plans in their minds that they lose track of their personal possessions, leaving their coats on planes and their umbrellas in restaurants. Personal possessions are a low priority for Loving Tans—a fact that causes dismay and anxiety in parents and mates. They also do not take care of their possessions, and they have little idea of what is required to maintain them. They buy boats without being aware of launching fees or marina rentals and without realizing that the hull will need to be scraped clean of barnacles once a year. The details—maintenance, upkeep, repair, taxes, and payment—have little or no meaning for a Loving Tan.

Loving Tans often overspend for items that others consider a luxury but that they consider a necessity. They make up the difference by skimping on the real necessities of life. Money, for a Loving Tan, is one of the hard facts of life; it is a fact they are not emotionally or mentally equipped to handle.

CAREER OPTIONS

Loving Tans do well in careers where they have personal autonomy with a minimum amount of supervision. They do well as landscapers, gardeners, groundskeepers, and in any other occupation that has its own internal harmony and rhythm.

Loving Tans truly love people and do well when they have an opportunity to be out in the community servicing the needs of others. Therefore, Loving Tans make good salespeople, customer service representatives, and consultants. They need to work for an organization rather than be self-employed, however, because they have a difficult time organizing the paperwork so as to keep their own business profitable.

Because of their ability to see an entire project all at once, they make good computer programmers. Their mechanical aptitude combined with their ability to start anywhere on a problem gives them the capability to debug programs. The more complex the problem, the better they like it.

Loving Tans have infinite patience, a love of knowledge, and the ability to teach those with curious minds and a will to learn. They make excellent mentors and teachers, especially in a research situation where many different outcomes are possible. They are content to discover nylon while searching for an antibiotic.

SPIRITUALITY

Eagerness, willingness, and optimism are the hallmarks of the Loving Tans' spiritual search. To them, every idea seems new and fresh. They explore the various concepts of spirituality the way children hunt for eggs on Easter morning, eagerly anticipating the excitement and involvement. In their search for meaning, Loving Tans willingly set aside the filters of preconception and experience, opening themselves to new ideas. However, they more easily accept ideas that are similar to their current belief system. If they are Jews or Christians, for example, they might find shamanism an interesting idea but not one they wish to explore.

Because of the Mental Tan component of their Personality Spectrums color, Loving Tans tend to be happiest with a theology or dogma that has an intellectual basis. Religions based on laws or principles appeal to Loving Tans. However, this applies only to the intellectual components of their belief system. When a religion attempts to impose a code of behavior on Loving Tans, they are likely to balk because they are unable to live within such a rigid structure. Loving Tans will leave a religion when they perceive that there is little flexibility and inadequate appreciation of the broad spectrum of human behavior.

Loving Tans love to spend time thinking, discussing, and writing about their spirituality, intellectualizing about their own and others' experiences. Therefore, they are always interested in spiritual experiences that have worked for other people, and they are fascinated by the techniques within a faith, such as prayer, and by the mechanisms that make the system work. Religions that offer opportunities to learn appeal to Loving Tans. Given a technique such as creative visualization or affirmation, they will begin using it immediately. Loving Tans will write hundreds of affirmations, placing them all over the house—on bathroom mirrors, refrigerators, and closet doors—to remind themselves to keep a positive outlook on life. But often, before they discover whether the affirmations work, they will attend another workshop, learn another technique, and go off on a whole new tangent.

Loving Tans see God as the critical parent, a power to be placated and feared. They have the hopeful relationship of a child to its parent, as if by being good they will earn some sort of merit. However, in the deepest recesses of their souls, Loving Tans desire to feel at one with God, to feel acceptance and love without judgment.

TWELVE

BLUE

Blues embody the characteristics of nurturing and care-taking. They are the Personality Spectrums color most concerned with helping other people. Whereas Nurturing Tans find their life's work in the community, Blues find value in being of service to individuals. Service is a form of altruism, a giving of oneself. It is the art of anticipating the needs of other human beings and ministering to those needs while at the same time allowing the individuals to maintain their dignity. In doing a kindness for a neighbor or performing an act of mercy for a patient, Blues feel fulfilled, valued, and of worth; they find ways to live their lives by giving.

The greatest challenge for Blues is to know what they need to be happy and then to ask for it. Because they are so caught up in service to others, Blues often spend too little time and attention on their own spiritual and emotional growth activities. They must set limits and boundaries on their emotional, physical, and spiritual resources; they must be able to say no and mean it. Blues need to emulate the wise cook who returns a portion of the starter dough to the yeast pot for another day. In this way, Blues can maintain their personal power. They must learn how to husband their own internal resources by measuring them out and using some of their time and energy to renew themselves.

APPROACH TO PHYSICAL REALITY

Blues do not find much to recommend physical reality. To them it is dirty, harsh, and ugly. Even an idyllic country scene viewed from a hilltop is, on close inspection, found to be alive with thousands of creepy, crawling bugs. Blues tend to live in the realm of emotions and feelings, which are more real to them than the external environment.

Left to their own devices, Blues do not particularly care for strenuous, sweaty physical activity or exercise. It makes them hot and sticky, a most unpleasant experience. However, they do enjoy sports that have a component of camaraderie, such as softball, volleyball, and bowling, or a component of grace and beauty, such as dancing, swimming, and horseback riding. They enjoy walking as a way of experiencing nature or being with friends out-of-doors. Exercise classes that incorporate gentle stretching, with a less hectic atmosphere than aerobics, appeal to Blues. Endurance sports requiring constant physical conditioning generally do not attract Blues, because they perceive that amount of attention to oneself as indulgent and narcissistic.

Blues tend to have an endomorphic body type—the "earth mother" figure. They put on weight easily, especially after the birth of children. In an era with so much emphasis on diet, exercise, slender figures, and no hips, Blues are at a disadvantage. Full-figured, especially after menopause, Blues need to understand that their beauty lies in their ability to nurture and support others and in their pleasing personalities.

MENTAL ATTITUDES

The Blues' greatest gift is their highly developed intuition. They are extremely sensitive to the emotional vibrations of others. However, it is extremely difficult for them to translate what they know intuitively into useful information. In the decision-making process, emotions, feelings, and hunches are not usually given equal weight with facts and figures. Therefore, Blues feel less adequate than other colors when it comes to making an intellectual contribution. The ability to collect, sort, store, and retrieve information is an acquired skill, one that Blues must learn, specifically through training in critical thinking.

Like all of the Emotional/Spiritual Colors, Blues are holistic thinkers. They grasp all the parts of a discussion or decision-making model simultaneously, juggling outcomes and the attendant consequences, assessing and evaluating cause and effect, always holding open the alternative options.

If a Green thinks in a binary manner, cutting and paring options at every choice point on the binary tree, a Blue mentally hangs on to the whole tree, never letting go of any of the potential options. Since Blues hold all the alternative solutions simultaneously in mind, it is no wonder they have a difficult time making decisions! Blues can get bogged down in

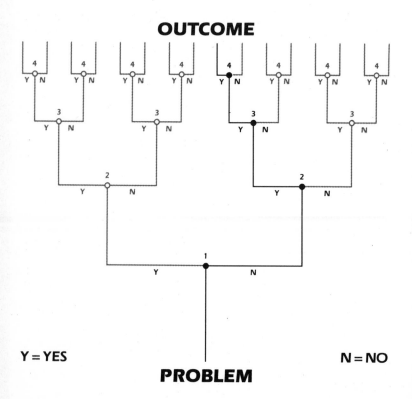

OUTCOME

Y = YES

N = NO

PROBLEM

the details and feel unsure of where they are going or how to proceed. The most important skill a Blue can learn is how to focus, to cut away all issues and concerns that do not have immediate pertinence to the problem at hand.

In school, Blues do well in subjects that place a high degree of emphasis on intuition or feelings: literature, creative writing, art, and drama. Those subjects requiring a linear approach, like mathematics or the hard sciences, teach the skills of memorization, organization, and building hierarchies. These are the subjects that assist Blues in learning to handle real-world data. It is frustrating for Blues to know the answer to a math problem and not know how they got it.

Although they are highly emotional, Blues can do well in business, especially those having a service component that allows Blues to work closely with other people. Blues are capable of making decisions; they are just slower and more deliberate than other colors. They lack the organizational ability of the Mental Tan or the Green, and the strong personal ego of a Violet.

Blues need to create schedules for coping with business situations, schedules that allow them sufficient time to work at their own speed. Blues need three to seven days to make a big decision. Given that time, space, and quiet, Blues make good decisions that are well thought out and to which they are committed. To be comfortable emotionally, they need to ask that all proposals and complaints be put in writing. This gives them an opportunity to separate the feelings from the action and to create a solution that they can support.

Blues weigh all of the factors that must be taken into consideration in any decision-making process: previous commitments, needs of family and self, the merits of the project, and the intended outcome. When confronted with employers and customers who demand instant decisions, Blues must be honest about their motives and requirements before they take any action. Blues take business setbacks personally. In the world of the Mental Family colors, everything is first an *idea*; in the world of Blues, everything is first an *emotion*. Acknowledging their feelings and being willing to keep moving in spite of them allows Blues to function successfully in the world of business.

The greatest asset a Blue has is emotional commitment. This is part of the Blues' mental and emotional process—they see the potential inherent in good ideas, and they want to help others achieve their goals. Any idea, project, or individual to whom a Blue is bound is indeed fortunate. A committed Blue is reliable, dependable, and trustworthy.

EMOTIONAL MAKEUP

Blue is the color of female energy and uniquely reflects one aspect of feminine energy—the ability to get in touch with and express one's feelings. Blues make sense of the world through their emotions rather than through physical sensations, as Yellows and Physical Tans do. Love, hate, hope, despair—these are everyday facts of life for Blues. Emotions are the data base on which they make decisions and take actions.

This ability to act from an emotional center is the Blues' greatest asset, but it can also be their greatest liability. They want to love and care for others and are perceived as loving, thoughtful, kind, and helpful. The liability comes when emotional confusion clouds the facts of a situation, preventing the Blues from making the best decisions. They are unable to discern, for example, the difference between being taken advantage of and being asked to give a little extra effort to achieve success.

Because they are so sensitive and pick up nonverbal cues to the moods of others, Blues are not acknowledged for what they know. Mates and employers, who use a more rational approach, ask what data the Blues have to support their opinion. Since the data are usually feelings, they are discounted as irrelevant, unspecific, or unscientific. In our society, the intuitive knowledge of a Blue is sometimes disconcerting and may seem irrelevant to those with a more mental outlook. However, in those areas of life where their specific gift is necessary, where nurturing and caretaking are essential to the continued well-being of the family and community, Blues are perceived as necessary and valuable.

Blues love people. To serve others is their life's work. A Blue's sense of well-being comes from tending to the needs of significant others. This caretaking can take the form of cooking, cleaning, and throwing parties, or of listening, accompanying a friend to the doctor, and giving advice. One of the hazards for a Blue is being taken for granted by family and friends. The truth is, they are! In their eagerness to help others, Blues open themselves to being used, failing to ask for repayment in kind. Blues assume that others are as sensitive as they are. The truth is that others don't see the Blues' needs and even if they do, they will let the Blues bear the burden. This leaves Blues feeling unappreciated for the effort they have made.

To combat this, Blues need to be much more assertive. They need to learn to set limits on their service, to communicate their expectations clearly (including monetary considerations), and to take action if their requests for gratification are not honored. In short, they must learn *assertive* communication skills. The more they allow themselves to be victimized, the more sorry they feel for themselves, which leads to a greater sense of futility. This downward cycle causes Blues to resort to a whole cycle of complaint, which sometimes leads to real and imagined illnesses, the most serious of which is the loss of self-esteem and respect.

Blues must learn that their needs are as important as the wants and needs of others. They must learn to nurture themselves, to give to themselves as generously as they give to others.

Blues need to nurture the emotional side of their personality. Activities that support this include keeping a journal, writing, reading, listening to music, enjoying quiet times alone or outdoors, being with friends, and *being listened to*. Without an opportunity to sort out their jumble of feelings, Blues find themselves in an endless morass of emotions without resolution.

Blues express their emotions through the language of laughter and tears, both of which bubble to the surface easily and quickly, much to the Blues' embarrassment. This is not an affectation, but rather the spontaneous release of pent-up emotion that, if kept inside, would cause physical problems like headaches.

Blues know intuitively that language is a poor medium of

expression for the rich depth and texture of what goes on inside them. They are touched deeply by sunsets, church music, and being with a loved one. When they and their partner have mated at the spiritual level, Blues are so overcome with the emotion of that experience that they express their joy and happiness in tears.

Blues also cry when they are angry. Contrary to popular opinion, Blues do not use tears as a manipulative device for getting their own way. When confronted with an angry spouse or employer, they should first express the emotion represented by the tears—anger, rage, frustration, helplessness, or betrayal. Only then can they move into a more rational discussion of the situation and search for alternative resolutions.

Blues understand that there is an underlying logic to what they are feeling. They cannot explain it; they can only feel the emotions. For them to ignore or disparage this aspect of themselves is to abdicate the source of their power. When in touch with their feelings, Blues are galvanized into action. For Blues, emotions are the coin of human interaction, without which there is nothing worthwhile.

SOCIAL STYLE

Blues love people and are loved in return. They enjoy caring for and helping others, often at their own emotional expense. As expressions of their love, they often put the needs of others ahead of their own. When appreciated and acknowledged for this contribution, Blues are at peace with themselves and at home in the world. They are happiest in their relationships with mates, children, and friends. Giving to those they love is not considered a sacrifice or a hardship to a Blue. Being unappreciated or taken for granted, however, will erode a Blue's capacity to serve.

Blues spend long hours planning activities, events, and gestures to express their love. Special meals, favorite activities, or full-blown birthday celebrations are some of the ways Blues communicate the depth of feeling they have for those they care about. Holidays are especially meaningful to Blues, especially those that fall at the end of the year. Being traditionalists, they love rediscovering favorite family decorations, preparing traditional meals, and experiencing the close warmth of family and home. Holidays without these components are cold, empty, and depressing: a time of year to be endured.

Blues love giving and receiving gifts. They choose gifts for others with thoughtfulness and care, often giving the gift of themselves in handcrafted items. Because Blues seem so down-to-earth, others often give them gifts that are practical or useful in the home. In truth, nothing thrills Blues like a gift they would not buy for themselves: expensive perfume, bubble bath in fancy containers, decorator items for the home.

Blues need to become more assertive. When they set limits on the emotional demands placed on them by family and friends, they are able to make better decisions. By realizing they have a right to be happy, they can protect themselves from being emotionally used up. The hardest lesson for Blues to learn is that they will have nothing to give others unless they first give to themselves.

COMPATIBILITY WITH OTHER COLORS

Physical (environmental) Colors

Blues and the Physical (environmental) Colors are a difficult mix. Reds, Oranges, and Magentas are hedonistic, physical, and spontaneous whereas Blues are introspective and intuitive. A Blue would prefer spending time cuddled up beside a warm fire, drinking tea and reading a book, whereas the Physical (environmental) Colors would prefer to be out-of-doors riding horses, backpacking, or roller-skating. Mating with someone in this family of colors would also cause the Blue to question whether the commitment was made out of lust or love.

Physical (body) Colors

Blues and Yellows both benefit by settling down early in life, but for different reasons. A Blue, before marriage, is like someone walking around with only one high heel on looking for the other shoe. They look at every mate as a potential life-partner. Yellows need to mate so that their sexual needs can be met within the loving confines of a secure emotional relationship. The bonding of a Blue and Yellow, then, is a relationship in which each partner's needs can be fulfilled.

Physical Tans are usually too intense, too withdrawn, too private, to meet the emotional needs of a Blue. Blues want to know what their mates are thinking and feeling, and Physical Tans may perceive their curiosity as intrusiveness. Therefore, the more the Blue demands from a Physical Tan, the more the Physical Tan withdraws and withholds affection and communication.

Mental Colors

Mental Tans and Blues make a nice predictable kind of couple. They combine steadfastness and dependability with a desire for emotional and financial security.

Greens become impatient with the interminable process that a Blue must go through in order to make decisions. Greens keep hoping that Blues will learn to speed up the process, but they never do. For a Blue, each new decision requires cataloging and retrieving data. Blues also do not have to have a reason for doing something. "Just because" is a perfectly good rationale. Greens, who pride themselves on their rationality, have difficulty living with the capriciousness of Blues and with their random thought process.

Nurturing Tans and Blues share warmth, compassion, and a genuine caring for people and causes. They are the kinds of couples who become house parents in juvenile homes, directors of summer camps, or tour guides. Out of their relationship with each other, they are renewed so that they are able to give to others.

Loving Tans have great compassion for the seemingly random emotional process of the Blue. They should. A Loving Tan thinks the way a Blue feels—every which way at once. The problem arises when decisive action must be taken and neither the Loving Tan nor the Blue is capable of, or willing to, exert leadership within the relationship. Each is looking for the other to take charge; consequently no one does, and soon bills are overdue, parking tickets remain unpaid, and neither can rectify the situation.

Emotional/Spiritual Colors

Very few men are Blues. However, when a Blue meets a Blue, there is an abundance of loving compassion, tenderness, and thoughtfulness. The problem arises when neither wants to hurt the other's feelings by exerting too much pressure or dominance within the relationship. Blues are very sensitive to other people's wants and needs, and in a Blue-Blue relationship, they are careful not to impose on their partner.

Violets and Blues are a dynamic duo. Because they are both in the Emotional/Spiritual Family of colors, they have similar wants and aspirations. The Violet is capable of envisioning a project big enough to keep both partners working a lifetime. Blues love to support that level of commitment to the future. The biggest problem is that Violets are not always sensitive about sharing the honors and the limelight. This causes Blues to feel unloved, unappreciated, and taken advantage of. They retaliate by withdrawing their love and support.

The problem with Blues and Lavenders together is that while Lavenders love the nurturing and the homey feeling created by the Blue, they do not want to be ensnared by it. Lavenders, in an effort to maintain their autonomy, will then feign indifference to their surroundings. Blues end up with hurt feelings. These two colors would get along better if they had separate homes and exchanged visits.

Crystals are the one Personality Spectrums color that has nothing to learn from a Blue and vice versa. When in relationship together, Crystals and Blues seem to affect each other like fingernails across a chalkboard. Blues are capable of keeping track of the needs of many people; Crystals become upset and nervous if too many demands are placed on them at one time. Blues love having many people come and go in their lives; Crystals need a great deal of quiet time. The timing and the needs of these two colors are in opposition.

Indigos benefit from the tolerant attitude of the Blues. However, Indigos are not as physically demonstrative as Blues need their mates to be. Indigos tend to be detached observers in the relationship, sometimes depriving Blues of closeness and physical intimacy.

PERSONAL POWER AND LEADERSHIP STYLE

Blues are the team leaders in life. They support, encourage, and facilitate others. Blues are most comfortable in a shared leadership role—that of co-captain or a first among equals. Blues will take on a chairmanship, divide the work equally among all the members, and include themselves as a member of the team, even lending an extra pair of hands when necessary.

The most difficult challenge for Blues is joint decision-making. Blues want to take other people's abilities, attitudes, values, and emotional needs into consideration. Consequently they spend too much time listening to the opinions and suggestions of others when faced with the need to make a decision. The goal of every Blue's decision-making process is consensus. Disagreement, loud arguments, and personality conflicts make life very difficult for the Blue leader.

FINANCIAL CHOICES

Since money matters are essentially accounting procedures, Blues have difficulty attaching emotions to finance. They feel that money is crass, and they do not like to discuss financial matters. In business, one of the hardest things Blues have to do is ask for money. People and personal interactions are important; money is secondary. Therefore, Blues need to make monetary agreements up front and in advance so that they will be free to interact emotionally, which is what they do best.

Blues are excellent stewards of someone else's money. They take the responsibility seriously. They are dependable, frugal, and cautious. In marriage or business, they see the money as belonging to someone else. Careful in spending and conserving the resources, they prefer not to take risks in the realm of high finances. Like Nurturing Tans, they choose safe investments like real estate as opposed to gambling on the stock market.

CAREER OPTIONS

Blues are such good listeners that they often become the unpaid counselors and therapists in the neighborhood. They are willing to listen to every detail of life's traumas and heartaches. But Blues find it difficult to remain objective and uninvolved, and soon they find themselves taking sides, becoming frustrated when there is no action. All too often, they find that they have simply been the sounding board for a chronic complainer who had no intention of doing anything about the problem. This emotional identification and lack of objectivity make it difficult for Blues to become therapists. They empathize too closely with the client.

Blues have traditionally regarded work outside the home as a second source of income, not necessarily as a tangible reward for their efforts and creativity. Consequently, they have often found themselves in jobs rather than careers, choosing traditionally female support positions as secretaries, nurses, and teachers. With more opportunities becoming available to women, Blues are moving out from this traditional stance, going into business for themselves. They are giving new, creative twists to traditional occupations, becoming nurse practitioners and consultants, and establishing new industries.

Blues are beginning to understand the economic clout of women, and they want to become a part of that dynamic. They make excellent personnel directors, accountants, customer service representatives, ministers, and seminar leaders. Because they believe in shared power, they do well in any occupation that has a built-in support team or consensus decision-making procedure. They do not do well in occupations such as law or contract negotiation, where they must mask their feelings. Nor do they operate well in isolation—as writers, for example—or in jobs where they must enforce rules that they had no say in formulating (such as jail guard or social service worker). They do well in service-oriented businesses like placing temporaries, doing bookkeeping and accounting, or performing personal grooming services.

If they decide to become entrepreneurs, they should either have a supportive mate or a partner who is willing to handle the legal and financial details of the business. Blues are so eager to help people that they frequently forget to charge their customers. Having someone else hold the bottom line is essential for a Blue.

SPIRITUALITY

Spirituality is the driving force of the Blues' life and their search for a deep, abiding relationship with God. To Blues, God is not an anthropomorphic being, a man sitting up in the clouds throwing down lightning bolts, but rather a loving, omnipotent power and guiding presence in their life.

The depth of their spirituality and their love of God is not something Blues can easily discuss with family or friends, for the emotions connected to their feelings for God do not translate easily. It is not based on theology or dogma, logic or reason. It is a feeling of love that is so profound that it renders Blues teary and speechless in awe and wonder. These tears are the hallmark of the deep, intense emotion a Blue has in uniting with God.

Blues have a strong sense of God. They experience, feel, and know God, as opposed to intellectualizing about the concept of God. To them, God is not an idea; God is real, experienced as love, comfort, and faith. As children, many Blues have had a transcendent experience of God. As a result, they know the God of Love. Many Blues do not feel that their religious experiences are given credence by others, nor do they receive the intellectual and spiritual support they feel they need. As a result, they spend much of their lives looking for a context, a religion, a system of beliefs big enough to hold what they have already known and experienced. Many Blues search for a spiritual home their whole lives, joining one religion after another, hoping to find understanding and a place to grow spiritually.

Participating in some form of organized spiritual practice is also an important experience for Blues. The setting is as important as the service, and they are profoundly moved by the ritual ceremonies. Music, candles, and prayers feed their soul. Holy places, no matter what religion has enshrined them, are mystical and magical for Blues. Blues can have profound spiritual experiences in their hometown church or at the top of Machu Picchu.

Blues have an abiding faith and trust in God. To them, God is a real and present force in their lives. No matter how bad things may be, Blues are able to call forth a sense of knowing that everything will be all right. Prayer for a Blue is active—a walk in the woods, quiet time at the sewing machine, or working alone on a project where they can be open to the ideas and inspirations that come. With their hands busy, their mind is free to roam, to contemplate the mysteries of life in all their wonder and complexity.

Blues constantly seek ways to be of service to family, friends, and neighbors because, to them, this is also a way to be in service to God. By giving of themselves to others, Blues feel they are giving back some of what they have received from God. For them, spirituality must also have a practical application.

THIRTEEN

VIOLET

Violets are the Personality Spectrums color that is most nearly aligned with the psychic, emotional, and spiritual balance in operation on the planet at this time. They have not only the opportunity but also the resources to make their lives count for something, to make a significant difference to our collective future.

The key that opens the door to a Violet's potential is the understanding that they are the visionaries of the world to come, the ones who can see the plants of tomorrow in the seeds of today. They need to understand their purpose and translate their abilities into action. They need to identify those changes in society that will have positive impact on our future, and they must then be willing to work toward implementing those changes.

The single most difficult thing for a Violet to do is to learn to live without guilt. This sense of guilt stems from the self-criticism that demands that the Violet do it better, faster, and now! This creates so much remorse, recrimination, and self-hate that a Violet is almost immobilized. The secret for Violets is to focus so clearly on the vision of the future that the mistakes and mishaps of today are diminished by the bright promises of the future.

APPROACH TO PHYSICAL REALITY

Violets are the theoreticians of the Personality Spectrums system. They are not concerned with the practical application of an idea, only with the inspiration behind it. Violets are not concerned with the nuts and bolts; they do not care how something works, only that it does.

Because Violets have so little feel for what it takes to make something happen in physical reality, they must depend on other people to help them create homes, environments, or products. Otherwise, their ideas remain half formed, stuck in the limbo of their minds. Violets assume that if they have seen it or envisioned it, the idea or product is right on the horizon ready to pop into being.

To others Violets may seem single-minded in their pursuit of monetary rewards and possessions, showing a strong connection to the world of the physical. Just the opposite is true. Violets are interested in money and possessions because they know that to make changes, one must have power. The possessions and money *represent* power and the ability to inspire and motivate others. Violets, left to their own devices, can live very frugally with few creature comforts; material things have no meaning for Violets, except as symbols.

MENTAL ATTITUDES

Violets are extremely intelligent. They are critical thinkers and have the ability to make generalizations and evaluations and to develop creative ideas. When generalizing, Violets will find the one piece of data that doesn't fit and then ask why until they have found the answer. In this way, they discover the key to the puzzle. By understanding what doesn't work, they discover new solutions, whether they are seeking innovative products, marketing new ideas, or generating alternative solutions to old problems. Violets always seem to see the big picture *and* its smaller components, the forest *and* the trees. Violets see and understand the concept of the forest from the example of each individual tree. Violets are always looking for the law or principle involved.

Violets have developed complex criteria by which they judge and evaluate the data of their lives. This attribute gives others the impression that Violets are hypercritical and fault-finding. Instead, they are expressing their frustration because others do not see the envisioned outcome as clearly as they do.

Research is one of their natural talents. Violets love the mental stimulation of the quest—following a single idea back to its source or forward to its conclusion. Violets are the theorists; they are interested in the hypothetical construct rather than the concrete applications. They are content to let others create the testing model. It is enough that they came up with the idea.

EMOTIONAL MAKEUP

Violets' emotions run deep; they seethe with passion. They may seem to have cold, aloof, arrogant exteriors, but these are only their defense against intrusion into their area of greatest vulnerability—their emotions. This Achilles' heel of Violets is the pathway to their soul, to the higher self that stands in awe of the challenge and mystery of their own lives. Violets seem strong, confident, and self-sufficient, when in fact, they are not. They doubt themselves. They have so often been ahead of their time, ridiculed, and made to feel out-of-step that they withdraw emotionally. They erect barriers of superiority and distance to protect themselves.

Emotionally speaking, Violets have a heightened sensitivity; they are very intuitive. They express their sexuality with deep passion. For a true sense of fulfillment, they must marry for both lust and love. Sexual communication is nonverbal, and they want sex itself to be on the deeper spiritual level. As lovers, they anticipate and determine their partners' sexual needs from their emotional vibrations. If a partner needs prolonged, sensual, tension-building foreplay, a Violet will intuit that without having to be told. Violets are jealous of anything or anyone that comes between them and their source of emotional security—even their own children. They are demanding mates and stern, rather autocratic parents.

Violets are capable and confident, with dynamic energy and a no-nonsense approach. They want to get things done. Violets who must carry the majority of responsibility in a relationship can experience a lot of anger. Violet women may have to resist an immense amount of social pressure that has attempted to force them into passive roles and behavior contrary to their strong dynamic natures. When forced by family or society into this passive stance, Violets take their anger out on themselves, often exhibiting driving, demanding behavior. They compensate by setting excessive standards of achievement for mates and children. This attachment to external standards at the expense of shared communication can drive an emotional wedge between Violets and their loved ones.

Violets can be very intense in their search for the emotional haven of a relationship. They form deep, sensitive attachments with mates, often relying on them to fulfill all their needs for affection. As loners, they prefer not to have to venture out into the world for sensory gratification. Therefore, mates provide all of the friendship, companionship, camaraderie the Violets should be getting from work, friends, and other social outlets. Violets can be very possessive, demanding, and selfish in their relationships.

SOCIAL STYLE

Violets are the oldest color in the spectrum. They seem to have an intuitive understanding of many ancient histories and experiences, which they draw upon to revitalize and renew themselves from within. The activities, ideas, and social interactions that are vital and necessary to other Personality Spectrums colors seem boring, or without social merit, to a Violet.

To others, especially mates, Violets appear to be antisocial. They tend to be distant, aloof, and somewhat cool in their relationships. They feel they have no time for idle chatter or social activities that they perceive to be time wasters. They want to engage in conversation at a significant level, and they dislike polite party chatter, preferring intense one-on-one conversations to large crowds or parties.

COMPATIBILITY WITH OTHER COLORS

Physical (environmental) Colors

While Reds and Violets seem to be at opposite ends of the Personality Spectrums system in every aspect of life, they are in fact two sides of the same coin. The physicality of the Red tempers and moderates the lofty idealism of the Violet, and vice versa. Violets feel safe with Reds because they know that the details of their physical existence will be taken care of, leaving Violets free to do the unencumbered thinking they do best.

Violets and Oranges repel one another because they are so similar. Both resist taking orders from anybody. Both require freedom of movement and self-expression—the Orange in physical reality, the Violet in the intuitive realms. The Orange disdains the Violet's vision; the Violet disparages the Orange's prowess and daredevilry. Should these colors mate, fireworks will be the order of the day.

Magentas are perceived by Violets as wacky and slightly off-center. Violets envision a golden city on a hill, and Magentas turn it into an amusement park. Magentas see Violets as puffed up with self-importance and pomposity, which Magentas are perfectly willing to prick with a pin. Only if Magentas are willing to tighten the reins on their imaginations, and if Violets are willing to loosen up a bit, can these two auras work well together.

Physical (body) Colors

Childlike Yellows and serious Violets are a combination with too many attributes in opposition. Yellows are spontaneous, playful, exuberant, and embrace life fully, while Violets are sober, dedicated, and weighted down with responsibility. The Violet resents the Yellow's playfulness; the Yellow chafes under the rules and regulations imposed by the Violet. These colors are unsuited for a union of equals.

Physical Tans have an innate quiet dignity about them that appeals very much to the serious-mindedness of the Violet. The physical, mental, and emotional independence of a Physi-

cal Tan relieves the Violet of the traditional caretaking responsibilities. By the same token, the independent nature of the
Physical Tan also precludes a lack of deep spiritual sharing
that is essential to a Violet's health and well-being within a
relationship. Again, not a good mix.

Mental Colors

Mental Tans and Violets come together to create unions
that function like partnerships. Each member is responsible
for specific areas of daily life. Mental Tans pay the bills,
organize the home, and set up schedules. Violets are responsible for creating and maintaining the romantic and sexual
excitement within the relationship as well as for setting the
tone of intellectual and artistic pursuits.

Greens and Violets create a dynamic duo. Give to a Green
a Violet's vision and the Green will make it a reality. Efficient,
productive, and well organized, Greens love creating the system for giving life to a Violet's vision. Because the Green is
sensual and sexual as well as intellectual, a Violet is intrigued
and enmeshed for life. Greens are also strong enough to avoid
being overshadowed by the strength of the Violet's personality
and ego.

Nurturing Tans are low-key mates for the strong, forceful
personalities of the Violets. Nurturing Tans demand loyalty,
fidelity, and gratitude for their faithful, loving service. They
are willing to unswervingly support their visionary Violet.

Loving Tans and Violets share many intellectual gifts.
They both love research and the hunt for the elusive answer.
However, over the long term, Violets will grow bored with the
constant confusion and unfocused direction of the Loving Tan.
Also, Loving Tans tend to love people with an open acceptance; Violets are much more closed, abhorring vast numbers
of people involved in their lives.

Emotional/Spiritual Colors

Blues and Violets do well when mated. Blues love having
the Violets' visionary picture of the future as a palette for their

time, talent, and energy. Violets bask in the loving support provided by Blues. A problem arises, however, when Violets become so focused on their own needs that they fail to consider those of the Blue. The Blue ends up lost in the relationship.

When a Violet is mated with a Violet, two very strong, dominant personalities attempt to occupy the same space. They must first work out a shared decision-making formula within the relationship. They are then free to focus their dynamic energies on making things happen in the larger arenas of life. Sexually, when people of this Personality Spectrums color mate, their souls sing.

Lavenders give Violets a great deal of space within the relationship; they do not demand time or attention, nor do they ask who is going to do the dishes. Lavenders prefer to be on a very loose leash, and Violets, when engrossed in their life's work, are just as happy to have that kind of loose relationship. Violets do not like clingy, demanding relationships; so Lavenders will suffice as their mates.

Violets, when mated with Crystals, are the dominant partner in the relationship. They focus their drive and determination on their ideas and projects, becoming very much a part of the world. The Crystal mate takes the more passive role, leaving the Violet to be the leader in the relationship.

Indigos and Violets tend to clash because the Violets are determined to dominate the relationship out of their strong, forceful willpower. Indigos, however, refuse to be dominated, choosing instead to deal with the anger vented on them by Violets when they are thwarted. Violets, under stress, tend to manipulate others, bending their will through persuasion and coercion. Indigos refuse to be manipulated under any circumstances.

PERSONAL POWER AND LEADERSHIP STYLE

Violets are leaders. The nature and strength of their leadership potential make them the most powerful color in the spectrum. Violets know how to align themselves with the life force of the universe to give impact to their ideas and desires.

Because Violets are so powerful, their leadership style tends to be autocratic and dictatorial. They lead by telling other people what to do. When they are working from the inspiration of a vision, few resent their didactic style. When they are not, however, their leadership style is one of domination, manipulation, and control. When Violets are inspired, others are open and receptive to their leadership. When less powerfully motivated, Violets are perceived as selfish and egotistical, and their leadership is resented and ultimately undermined.

Violets tend to feel guilty about their leadership style, since it conflicts with social norms. The most difficult thing for Violets to understand is how others will take orders when they themselves would resent and resist that same autocracy. Violets need to understand that their leadership is not resented when they have chosen an outcome that inspires and motivates others to become better people with high ideals and hopes for the future.

To be successful leaders, Violets must balance the needs of their ego, that part of their personality which demands recognition and reward, against the demands of their soul, the higher self, which only wants to unite with God.

The positive ego, the part of the self that works for reward and gratification, establishes goals that allow the personality to determine how successful it is. The ego also protects us from being inundated with data, serving as both a motivator and a cosmic filter.

The deeper ego needs of most Violets are the intangibles—power, status, emotional security, and the ability to make things happen, to inspire and motivate others, to be a catalyst for change. The driving force behind most Violets is the need to make a contribution—to give something worthwhile to their community, industry, business, or church. They love to inspire and motivate others; they want to feel that they have affected the wider group; and they need to be recognized for their contributions. If all of these needs are met, the Violet is fulfilled and satisfied.

A secondary ego need of the Violets is to prove that there is something—an idea or universal force—larger than themselves. Violets feel that, by achieving their vision, they prove that this force or power is present, that worlds can be breached and that we can create our own reality. Violets who are willing to be the visionary leaders we so desperately need are in a position to lead us into the future.

The Violet has a strong positive ego counterbalanced against a strong soul connection to God. Both aspects are important, and the balance between the two creates a dynamic tension within the Violet personality. For a Violet, this fertile tension, this potential to be a change agent for the future, makes life worth living.

FINANCIAL CHOICES

Violets know how to acquire money with relatively little effort. More than any other Personality Spectrums color, they know how to work less and get paid more. Because Violets are basically lazy, they prefer making money without having to do physical work for it. To them, thinking is work and ideas are intellectual property.

Violets are not generous or free and easy with their money; they are the most selfish of all the colors. They are masters at fumbling for the check. If someone else offers to pick it up, a Violet will let them, even if the Violet is better able to pay.

In choosing a gift, Violets will carefully weigh all the factors before deciding how much to spend—the nature and duration of the friendship or relationship, the importance of the occasion, what they will get in return, and whether or not the size, price, and thoughtfulness of the gift will be noticed. Violets also tend to buy what they think the other person should have rather than what the person really desires. Violets are apt to give a book on their favorite topic in order to educate the recipient rather than a personal item that would make the person's heart sing. This habit originates out of the Violets' fear that someone will ask them for more than they are willing to give, a parsimoniousness of spirit.

On the other hand, Violets deny themselves nothing in the way of material possessions. They are not conspicuous consumers so much as deliberate, uninhibited consumers who buy exactly what they want. Nothing less will do.

Violets are very intuitive about money. They seem to sense where the jobs are, where to find the new opportunities for financial windfalls, and what new products or services will be the next fad or craze. They need to pay strict attention to their hunches. When they try to figure it out logically, they often miss their big chance because the element of fear has been introduced into the formula. When Violets see potential, they do not see a path fraught with disasters or calamities; they only see the outcome, the finished product, the success. When Violets listen with a keen inner ear attuned to their own experience, they always seem to know where the mother lode is buried—be it in real estate, new product development, design, or a fad.

CAREER OPTIONS

Violets have several skills and abilities that open up broad possibilities within the realm of work.

Violets love to tell other people what to do. When they can temper this didactic quality they make excellent teachers, trainers, ministers, public speakers, and actors. When they deliver motivational material, they are truly inspiring. They make excellent journalists and broadcasters because they not only see the day-to-day events but are also able to weave them into a congruent tapestry of the whole story.

Because they are able to see so many possibilities in the future, they do well at the senior level of management. They have the skills for setting policy as well as the ability to delegate the responsibility for implementing these policies. They do particularly well when put in charge of new products divisions or research and development.

Violets tend to be successful in professions like medicine and law, where there is a great deal to know or where there are many subspecializations within the same profession. Violets seem to learn intuitively, and once they have a feel for their subject, they have a holistic sense of its scope and of how information falls within its perimeters. It is as if they have a mental template that helps them assimilate information within a particular area of study.

Because Violets love to dwell in the realm of theory as opposed to the hustle and bustle of the everyday world, they do well in professions that have an element of creativity and that offer independence and time alone. They make good research scientists, operating in the realm of theoretical supposition. They also do well as artists and writers, because they are comfortable with the long hours of solitude with only the creative process for company. They do well in occupations that require the ability to project outcomes based on limited input—economic or social forecasting, advertising, and copywriting. They also make good inventors, designers, and innovators.

SPIRITUALITY

Violets perceive spirituality to be the wheel of spiritual growth and development. To them, spirituality means coming to terms with the nature of their own souls, fulfilling their individual destinies. Every Violet feels as if he or she has made a covenant, a sacred promise, that must be fulfilled. This places a moral weight on them. Many Violets are reluctant to acknowledge the power of the spiritual force in their life or consciously to choose to act out of it.

Some Violets consider spirituality to be an individual's personal relationship with God, or the communication one has with the Higher Power. Others define it as the ethical or moral tenets by which they choose to live. All Violets, however, are aware of a deep connectedness that goes beyond thoughts and words.

Violets understand that there is some Higher Power or Higher Law. They seem to recognize intuitively that inner place within themselves where God *always* is. The idea of God in a long white robe sitting on a cloud is incomprehensible to them, since they subscribe to a much broader concept of spirituality. Although Violets may belong to an orthodox religion, they always feel free to hold their ideas separate from the collective beliefs. Laws, theology, and dogma are meaningless to Violets. Instead, they listen to, understand, and obey the laws of the universe because they comprehend the concept of "oneness," retribution, or karma.

Violets are the visionaries of the Personality Spectrums system. A visionary is one who can experience or imagine an outcome in its totality before any tangible evidence indicates that it is even a possibility. Most Violets can envision a completed city where everyone else sees only an empty pasture. It is the bane of Violets' existence to be asked to explain what they know to be real or true when there is no evidence to give credence to that knowledge.

There is a distinct difference between a Violet who is a visionary and other colors that have creative abilities. The visionary sees the outcome in the mind's eye with power and clarity. Unlike the dreamer, who is satisfied simply to entertain an idea without being impelled to bring it forth, the Violet sees the concept complete, whole, finished, ready to be made concrete, tangible, real.

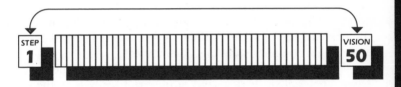

To be labeled a visionary calls forth a Violet's deepest self-doubts. "Why me?" the Violet may ask. "I'm not qualified. I don't know enough. I am too old. Or not old enough." Violets must confront several considerations when they accept the obligation of their personality color:

1. Their vision is bigger than they are. Nothing in their experience has prepared them for the scope or the audacity of the idea that they have. The image, picture, or concept seems to be beyond the scope of their background or education.

2. They are awed and humbled by the audacity of the vision. They feel inadequate to accomplish the task because they feel they lack the formal background, education, expertise, or financial support.

3. They feel compelled to do it. They feel they have no choice. No matter how long they have procrastinated or avoided the responsibilities, they have discovered that this "job" is theirs.

4. They have an inner drive to contribute to the world in a significant way. While Violets have strong personal egos, this urge goes beyond their need for recognition and glory.

The vision that ferments in the soul of a Violet has as its primary goal the betterment of the community through contribution to a major endeavor such as law, medicine, education, or government. The vision of a Violet can be so specific as to benefit only the neighborhood, or so large as to benefit the world. Most Violets become impatient with themselves when they see the potential for worldwide impact but cannot get their concept out of a city council subcommittee meeting.

To be fulfilled, Violets know deep within themselves that they must attempt to realize their vision in spite of the obstacles: self-doubt and fear; ridicule and loneliness. Once they surrender to being the vehicle for social change, they accept the personal and spiritual challenges and the opportunities for growth that are inherent in this commitment.

When Violets begin to act upon their vision, they are happy, productive, loving, and in tune spiritually with themselves and the universe. Violets in such a harmonious state know God and have direct access to greater wisdom. Violets' spiritual well-being is directly tied to their ability to identify and connect with the soul's work. Violets *must* give to society from a deep level within themselves. They have a strong desire to make their mark on the world, to have their lives count for something. They feel they have no choice about implementing the changes they see as necessary. They *know* that they have something worthwhile to contribute—to community, industry, business, or church.

The essence of the Violets' service is creating changes in the nature and makeup or thinking of the group or ideology with which they are involved. They carry within them a tension that gives them no peace, but that guides and directs their lives. If ignored, this tension makes it impossible for them to live at peace. Violets who have chosen to live out their lives in safe mediocrity tend to become angry and embittered, as if they know that they have chosen security at the expense of contribution.

Violets who resist living the visionary life harbor a secret unhappiness; their existence is tinged with anger, guilt, and grief. When they persistently refuse to acknowledge this motivation emanating from within, they set themselves up to be severely disappointed in life because they knowingly have failed to keep their covenant with God.

FOURTEEN

LAVENDER

Dreamer, drifter, fantasizer—these are the words that best describe the Lavenders. They first see the shifting layers of shape, form, and pattern that make up designs. The Lavenders dissolve and recombine these designs to create new structures and concepts. To see what a Lavender sees one must seek out bird shapes in the clouds and divas in the garden. With heightened abilities to see other dimensions within their mind's eye, Lavenders are open to exploring alternate realities—the realities that exist in science fiction and dreams.

The challenge for Lavenders is to stay in this, our reality, physically and emotionally. For them, it is much easier to live in the world of fantasy than to coexist with modern technology. Lavenders need to develop ways of using the images, ideas, and themes they experience in their dreams and fantasies to create a rich new fabric of legend, fable, and art for others.

APPROACH TO PHYSICAL REALITY

Lavenders tend to be less physical than other colors. They carry with them an aura of fragility, and they cope less well with the demands of tactile reality. They may even look pale and wan. Because they prefer the activities of a sheltered environment, they are not outdoor people, preferring to be inside, away from the hot sun and the cold rain. The reality of nature is difficult for them to appreciate emotionally. Abstractly, they can see the beauty in the earth, plants, insects, and the life cycle. Realistically, they find that digging is a dirty job, plants are the source of stains and unpleasant odors on their hands, and insects are repellent. They prefer an artistic depiction of nature to the harsh reality of it.

Lavenders seem to drift through life, making plans but never bothering to figure out what it would take to make them work. They have good intentions about redecorating the living room. But the task of driving to the store, making the color selection, and getting the paint home is so overwhelming that the Lavender may let the paint sit and never get around to putting it on the walls. By the time the Lavender is in the mood to paint, he or she will be tired of the color and will have to start the entire process over again. It is easier simply to think about redecorating the living room.

Lavenders have little sense of the relationship between time and space. They start out for the grocery store and end up in a town thirty miles away, having forgotten why they ever left home. They make appointments they never keep, or show up for them on the wrong day. They may invite friends for dinner and then make other plans for themselves that evening. Guests arrive and find that the evening's entertainment is a do-it-yourself dinner party.

Lavenders are not being rude or even thoughtless; they simply have difficulty, a kind of jet lag, adjusting to the differences between their fantasy lives and their real lives. They seem caught in a permanent dream world. To demand their attention and concentration is to ask them to pay close attention to this reality. That is not only difficult for a Lavender to do; it is also painful. They feel as if they are constantly getting jerked back into reality, the way others feel when someone keeps waking them up just as they drift off to sleep. This form of awakening is physiologically hard on the body's defense system; in a more extreme form this technique has been used to torture political prisoners. When friends and family become too insistent, demanding that Lavenders be responsible and dependable, the Lavenders can become angry and agitated. They only want to escape this reality; they only want some time and solitude with their images and their dreams.

MENTAL ATTITUDES

Lavenders have intuitive thinking skills as opposed to the logical, orderly, intellectual thinking common to the Mental Personality Spectrums colors. Lavenders make random connections among the items in the storehouse of information in their brain. This willingness to play with ideas, thought-forms, and mental pictures is the fountain of their creativity. It represents their willingness to go beyond what is accepted by society as the normal limits of creativity, opening new vistas for study and exploration.

Lavenders always begin with the premise, "Why not?" Because Lavenders live in the land of dreams and fantasies, they are not limited or confined by constraints of time, space, materials, technology, or budget. To them, all things are possible. This mental process is similar to, but not the same as, that of the Violet. Violets feel that they must be able to give life to an idea, product, or concept that is useful and practical and that points to the future. Lavenders do not make such demands on themselves. To them, the fact of having the dream or fantasy is enough. The most difficult part of life for a Lavender is having to act on the ideas that proliferate in their minds. Lavenders must work diligently to capture the will-o'-the-wisp ideas, must twist and spin and translate them into this reality the way a seamstress licks a piece of thread so the strands will go through the eye of the needle.

Lavenders have a gift for mentally holding on to the whole pattern of creative thought while simultaneously moving and shifting the various pieces to test various outcomes. They are able to move their point of focus, shifting at will from the minute details to the overall picture. This is a complex gift, one that often goes unrecognized and unrewarded in a society that admires practical, pragmatic thinking.

This ability to see patterns is shared by two other Personality Spectrums colors—Magenta and Green. Magentas see patterns in three-dimensional reality; they have the ability to cut and drape a pattern on a dress form or to create an architect's scale model. Greens, on the other hand, see patterns through time; they organize information for clarity and efficiency, creating time lines, flow charts, and schedules, all without having seen the finished product.

Lavenders see a pattern through space. This means that once they have seen it in their mind's eye, they have no need to reproduce it. In fact, their greatest challenge is to keep working until what they see in their head matches what they are able to reproduce tangibly.

Most often, Lavenders are best able to use their gift through the written word. As they picture in their minds the workings of a problem, it is translated into word pictures, rich with tonal, sensory texture. They have the language of the poet combined with the passion and dedication of an artist. Anything they can conceive in their mind's eye is a possibility, even those things which we do not yet have words to describe or explain.

Lavenders are primarily visual. The pictures they see, however, are truly multisensory experiences. Therefore, while many Lavenders are gifted visual artists, that medium alone is unable to convey the other sensory dimensions of their ideas and thoughts. Lavenders turn their attention then to their writing skills, developing a broad vocabulary to describe in minute detail nuances of emotion, feeling, person, place, and experience. Through the written word they make the fanciful appear real, giving it depth, perspective, and dimension.

Lewis Carroll and C. S. Lewis were both Lavenders who gave free rein to their creative energy through their writings. Lewis Carroll created a fantasy land where Cheshire cats disappear leaving only their smiles hanging in midair, and where a little girl named Alice is invited to a tea party at which there is no tea and everyone talks nonsense. C. S. Lewis created the *Narnia* series of children's stories in which altered time-space relationships were explored.

EMOTIONAL MAKEUP

This Personality Spectrums color is emotionally, psychically, and spiritually the least well grounded of all the colors. Lavenders seem to come into this reality cut adrift from anything that might give structure or meaning to their lives.

They have difficulty creating and maintaining a system of values and beliefs, and often adopt the guidelines of other, stronger personalities as their own.

Lavenders go through life as if they don't really belong, as if they don't fit in. They find it difficult to call any one place home. They feel out of sync and tend to shield themselves behind an opaque veil. When confronted by others who need specific information, Lavenders often retreat into a wide-eyed innocence that says, "Are you talking to me?"

Lavenders are the dreamers of the spectrum, and they indulge in all forms of self-induced altered states of awareness. They constantly daydream, sometimes drifting away in the middle of a sentence, caught up in the action they see in their minds. The words we speak can flip a switch in the Lavender's mind, releasing a flood of internal images. We on the outside are unaware of the Lavender's internal television. But, for the Lavender, what's going on inside his or her mind is so rich, external reality seems superfluous.

In addition to daydreams, they have vivid imaginations that enhance their propensity for autosuggestion (hypnosis), creative visualization, night dreams, and nightmares. Because they are so physically and emotionally sensitive, they can also experience clairaudience (the ability to perceive and understand sounds without actually hearing them), clairvoyance (the ability to perceive things that cannot be seen), and clairsentience (the ability to physically sense things that happen to another person, sometimes over a great distance). Lavenders place no restrictions on the internal mechanisms of their mind and are open to such experiences as automatic writing and other extrasensory phenomena.

Emotionally, Lavenders are not available for deep committed relationships with other people. Mates and children need to understand that Lavenders will express their love and caring in an offhand, casual way. Often they seem to their families to be uninvolved with the details of daily life. Lavenders care, but they are unable to express concern the way others want and expect them to. The mundane, humdrum activities of everyday life bore Lavenders and lead them to escape into their own heads for emotional and mental renewal.

Lavenders have difficulty establishing and maintaining deep levels of human interaction. Part of a Lavender is always on hold, unavailable to other people for close, warm interaction. Ultimately, to become enmeshed in the intricacies of a relationship would require that Lavenders relinquish that part of themselves that needs the freedom to explore the outer limits of their imaginations and their creativity.

In a society such as ours, which places so much emphasis on caring and nurturing, adult Lavenders have a difficult time conforming to the role of loving, caring, and nurturing mate and parent. They give all they have to give, but they are aware that they are incapable of giving as much or as easily as other Personality Spectrums colors. In their imaginations, they can see what they should do, but in reality they are unable to live it. This gives them a feeling of guilt tinged with a sense of inadequacy. Lavenders who have been unable to balance their inherent nature with their sense of guilt often withdraw emotionally and physically.

Lavender children who have the same problem escape into self-generated fantasy lands, creating imaginary friends and playmates for comfort and companionship. The positive gift these children have is a lively, quick imagination capable of opening horizons of creative play for others.

Lavenders are born with an active imagination and with the ability to create new and different realities; if not always practical, they are always interesting, providing food for thought for others.

SOCIAL STYLE

Socially, Lavenders tend to be loners, afraid that others will not understand their way of living. They live in their heads and seldom express what goes on in their minds for fear of being ridiculed, criticized, or ostracized. Therefore, Lavenders often develop compensating behaviors designed to make others think they are conforming to social norms when, actually, they are only concerned with creating an acceptable and unremarkable appearance that will protect their autonomy. For example, many Lavenders know how to appear to be paying attention when, in fact, their minds are a million miles away.

Lavenders are not caught up in a struggle with the ego, as Violets are. They do not value those things most of us feel are important or necessary in life. They want recognition for the artistic merit of their work. They are disciplined in the pursuit of their ideas, but they do not act just to make a social statement. They create because an idea has formed in their heads.

Lavenders have loose ties with their families and a few close friends. Of all the Personality Spectrums colors, Lavenders have the least need for the physical and emotional nurturing provided by these relationships. Instead, they prefer solitude with time for daydreaming. Lavenders become actively involved with their mental lives; their creations—whether paintings, writings, or some other form of artistic expression—have a life of their own. These creations become a Lavender's children, friends, and family.

Sexual expression is one area in which Lavenders can act out in this world what they see in fantasy. They are among the most sexually creative, the most willing to experiment, of all the Personality Spectrums colors. However, Lavenders do place limits on sexual exploration beyond which they will not travel. These limitations are based on their need for emotional and psychic safety. Their taboos and restrictions are self-imposed psychological and physical safety nets that don't necessarily conform to the taboos of a sexually inhibited society.

In a relationship where they feel emotionally and physically secure, Lavenders are creative, inventive, daring, and experimental, willing to be engaged physically so that their minds are free to roam the astral airwaves. It is as if Lavenders slip out of this reality while making love, knowing that their partner and their own bodies will remind them to come back.

COMPATIBILITY WITH OTHER COLORS

Physical (environmental) Colors

While Reds have an interest in sex compatible with Lavenders, they are too practical and realistic to appeal to the gentler Lavender. Lavenders want to lie in the sun and watch the clouds change shape while Reds want to be doing something. Lavenders are content to daydream, Reds want to interact with things. While they have a common meeting ground, there is little to sustain a deep, abiding mated relationship.

Oranges are willing to give Lavenders all the time and space they need or want, so much so that it is difficult to imagine how these two colors could work out a relationship. Oranges need to be fiercely independent, and Lavenders do not want to be restricted in their alone time. If these two colors cannot negotiate when they will both be home, there is little basis for a relationship.

Magentas share aspects of the Lavenders' creative process, which makes them more tolerant and understanding of the ways Lavenders function in the world. Neither color wants to be tied down emotionally. Because they both understand the need for individual autonomy, a Magenta and a Lavender can create a relationship together that will work well for both of them.

Physical (body) Colors

Yellows are compatible with Lavenders because they are emotionally safe, playful lovers who enjoy sex. Yellows are like enthusiastic children, willing to jolly a Lavender back into this reality the way a mother coaxes a smile from a cranky child after a nap. Yellows are enthusiastic playmates for Lavenders.

Physical Tans, like Reds, are too pragmatic and realistic to suit the dreamer aspect of the Lavender. While the Physical Tans' virility and inner strength appeal to a Lavender, their inability to communicate leaves a Lavender without anyone to talk to. Physical Tans are unable to operate within the realm of fantasy that is so important to a Lavender.

Mental Colors

Mental Tans are fascinated and attracted by the Lavenders' thinking process, which to a Mental Tan seems exotic and creative. Lavenders appreciate the methodical nature of the Mental Tan and recognize the need for one partner to make all the mundane decisions. If the Mental Tan is willing to hold a Lavender loosely within the relationship, not demanding adherence to a strictly defined role, then both could benefit within the marriage or partnership.

Greens probably make better business partners than mates with Lavenders, because Greens can see the value of many of the Lavenders' ideas and concepts. Greens get excited by the potential they see within the Lavenders, not realizing that Lavenders create only when they are moved by the spirit and not because there is a deadline. Sometimes, in their need to stay on schedule, Greens can ride roughshod over the emotional and spiritual needs of a Lavender, which causes havoc in a mated relationship.

Nurturing Tans are emotionally low-key enough to appeal to Lavenders. However, home, family, and community activities are very important to the Nurturing Tan. Though they see their partner as an equal participant in these activities, a Lavender is constricted by them.

Loving Tans and Lavenders both tend to get scattered when trying to hold together all the pieces of their lives. In a relationship, each will assume the other was taking care of the social calendar, groceries, and bills when, in fact, no one is taking care of the details of their lives. While they are both well-meaning, neither has the focus or inclination to make these tasks a priority.

Emotional/Spiritual Colors

Blues and Lavenders are emotionally sympathetic to one another. However, Blues need secure ties and emotional stability within a relationship. Lavenders want to be able to come and go as they please, and they also seek a level of grounded-ness and decisiveness that Blues usually cannot provide. Both colors would depend on their partners to give the relationship definition and direction.

Violets provide Lavenders with the ballast they need to navigate the shoals of life. Violets are capable of making the space emotionally and spiritually for a Lavender; they provide a strong homing signal that guides the Lavender back from that internal fantasy land. Violets intuitively understand what motivates and directs the Lavenders, and Lavenders can feed the Violets' visionary capacity by spinning tales of the future.

When Lavenders are mated to Lavenders, each partner expects the other to be responsible for the details of daily life. In this pairing, both partners are looking for the escape hatch into the stratosphere of their own inner worlds.

Crystals take the Lavenders' products, ideas, and fanta-sies, and convert them into objects of worship because they see so much ethereal beauty in them. Crystals appreciate the gentle nature of the Lavender, while the Lavenders appreciate the inner quiet that is so much a part of a Crystal's soul. Lavenders understand that the Crystal does not want to own them body and soul, and therefore make themselves emotion-ally and physically available to the Crystal.

Indigos and Lavenders respect each other's abilities and way of thinking. Lavenders, more closely than any other Personality Spectrums color, understand the true inner nature of the Indigo and refuse to be put off by those attributes or characteristics that others might find unusual. Lavenders and Indigos can create a relationship that allows both of them the freedom they need and the emotional security they want.

PERSONAL POWER AND LEADERSHIP STYLE

Lavenders are not leaders. It takes all they have to keep themselves on the right course in life; taking on the responsi-bility of showing others what to do is beyond them. They have neither the physical nor the emotional resources to be respon-sible to or for anyone else. However, this loner mentality ideally suits the Lavenders' purpose in life—which is to visit other realities, observing and reporting what they see, hear, and experience. If Lavenders tried to fit into the traditional model for success of modern society, their attempts to conform would stifle their ability to move, mentally, into other realms of thought.

Their very need to be alone is the source of the Lavenders' power. To have the courage to be different, to be unwilling and unable to conform, is the strength of a Lavender. Because they have often been misunderstood and criticized, they know that the greatest challenge for them is to stay in this reality when their presence is required here. For them, escape from the physical body and material world is easy; staying here is difficult and often physically painful. The goal for them is to return to this reality and report what they have experienced and seen in their mind's eye.

FINANCIAL CHOICES

Lavenders are like children when it comes to money. They have little or no concept of money as an idea, a medium of exchange, or a yardstick for measuring success. When they have it, they spend it. When they don't, they don't. For a Lavender, money is like a game. At the end of the game, the one with the most money wins. However, Lavenders frequently get bored and mentally drift away from the game before the outcome has been determined, leaving the other players with a hollow victory. Lavenders do not quit; they simply leave.

CAREER OPTIONS

Lavenders do best in situations where they can provide for themselves with a minimum expenditure of time and thought. Teaching, preferably at the university level where fewer emotional demands are made, will suit many Lavenders. Others will choose painting, writing, or some other creative pursuit that can provide them with a skeletal structure, giving them someplace to check in but leaving them with large blocks of time alone for the thinking and daydreaming that will allow them to create. Deadlines and responsibilities to editors or students can provide the Lavender with a reasonable impetus for finishing his or her work.

Lavenders do well in the performing arts, because this field provides them with a way to visit other realities naturally and authentically. When Lavenders are acting, they are living the part, becoming, in the flesh, that character. As dancers, they become the music. As mimes, they actually create a reality that the audience must otherwise imagine. Lavenders also do well behind the scenes in the theatrical world because there, too, they can live out their fantasies. Lavenders make good costume designers, set designers, and stage managers. The theater is an ideal field for Lavenders.

Lavenders do well as therapists in treatment centers where creativity and experimentation are encouraged. They make good art therapists and work well with people who have experienced some sort of paranormal phenomenon, especially in the context of spiritual growth and development. Clinical situations, however, are too rigid and stifling for the gentle laissez-faire style of a Lavender.

SPIRITUALITY

A Lavender's concept of spirituality is a cross between the mystical, magical fantasy of the Arthurian tales and the utopian futuristic societies of science-fiction stories. Lavenders do not hold themselves hostage to any one set of spiritual beliefs. They freely investigate any notion or concept that captures their interest.

God, to a Lavender, is a good idea, one which, in theory, they are willing to investigate. Yet anything that confines or circumscribes the parameters of a Lavender's reality—the rigid concept of God in the Judeo-Christian ethic, for example—they ignore or hold in distain. Any system of belief based on rules, regulations, or a code of behaviors is anathema to Lavenders. Conversely, free-thought movements that espouse individual, personal freedom appeal to these people. They want the opportunity to find the Higher Being in their own way and in their own time.

For Lavenders, a place of worship that is artistically beautiful is a source of spiritual inspiration and insight. Music, stained-glass windows, bells, incense, vestments, and candles all become the auditory, visual, and kinesthetic cues that give Lavenders permission to "go away," to freely enter the dream state they prefer to reality. In this state, the reality of worship and the tapestry of their inner mind overlap, creating a religious or spiritual experience that is rich in texture, color, harmony, and imagery. The visions may be awesome, but they are not necessarily mystical experiences in the traditional sense because Lavenders do not willingly give anyone, even God, power over them.

Lavenders best understand the world of magic and Merlins, where strict cause-and-effect relationships undergo alchemical changes, altering everything else in the process. This is not to say that Lavenders delve into magic or witchcraft—only that they understand intuitively the primary forces in those practices. They are not disciplined enough to be mystics or medicine men and women. They are the free spirits who come, sample, and take what they need from each system. The concept of God is hazy and ill defined for most Lavenders, although they have had powerful experiences that they might see as being "near God." Never knowing where their imagination will take them next, they are reluctant to say they have found *the* definite answer, the God of *all*.

In an attempt to find spiritual groups with whom they can identify, Lavenders try everything. They meditate in ashrams, chant bhajans, and eat macrobiotic food. They spend a great deal of time and energy looking for groups or ideologies that support and encourage their natural, intuitive process. Unfortunately, each system has an underlying structure of beliefs or dogma to which Lavenders are unwilling and unable to conform.

FIFTEEN

CRYSTAL

Crystals are natural healers. They utilize energy to transform light into healing rays. They become the medium or the conduit through which healing passes. They are able to increase their personal, physical power to the point where they are able to cleanse the minds and souls so that physical healing can follow.

Their biggest challenge is learning how to cope with the gift of healing. In order not to attract attention to themselves, Crystals become the chameleons of the spectrum, assimilating other colors into their aura in order to hide or protect themselves. They clutter up their own energy field when they do this, bringing harm to themselves. This act also confuses others. The challenge for Crystals is to learn to know themselves and what their special gifts are so that they do not have to disguise themselves through emotional camouflage.

APPROACH TO PHYSICAL REALITY

Crystals perceive the physical environment as harsh, unfriendly, and cold. It is physically painful for a Crystal to look at anything that is ugly, dirty, or unattractive. They are physically sensitive to noise and other kinds of pollution. They wish the world could be like the pristine palaces of their dreams and fantasies. When it is not, they are horrified.

Crystals, in their attempt to create in the real world the perfection they see in their minds, become obsessed with cleanliness and neatness. For example, in their homes they create an environment of hardwood floors, uncluttered spaces, and plain, simple furnishings. There is little that is sentimental about Crystals; therefore, they display only those reminders of family and friends that are truly meaningful to them.

Crystals often have the physical feeling of being fractured, and are therefore jealous of their private space. They allow only close and intimate friends or family to visit. They do not open their homes for large gatherings because they are uncomfortable with groups of people invading their space. They are much more comfortable with small, intimate groups for short periods of time.

To heal themselves, Crystals often find working the soil satisfying and stabilizing. Gardening, tending houseplants, or growing and drying herbs give Crystals a sense of emotional and physical satisfaction they seldom get from any other activity. It also provides them an abundance of quiet, serene time alone with God and nature, a necessity for their proper mental, spiritual, physical, and emotional balance.

A one-on-one healing situation is ideal for a Crystal, whether the Crystal is a therapist, counselor, or medical practitioner. Crystals have the ability to take the energy that flows into their body and direct it to others, healing the psyche and the soul. As a quartz crystal in a watch amplifies the electromagnetic energy within it to tell perfect time, so those with the Crystal Personality Spectrums color have the potential to amplify the dynamic force that flows through them. The Crystals' power is dynamic and secret; part of their personality pattern is to protect and nurture these healing gifts.

MENTAL ATTITUDES

Crystals are bright, quick, and mentally agile. They are avid readers and enjoy television, movies, and the theater, the main sources of social learning for a Crystal. They are essential because they provide clues to appropriate behavior, clues that Crystals need. They prefer books that give them an insight into the manners and morals of contemporary society; escapist literature is not for them. They also choose inspirational books—letters, diaries, prayers, philosophy, poetry, and biographies of leaders and teachers.

Crystals spend a great deal of time thinking about what they believe in, meditating and praying over the details of their life. But few Crystals would consider themselves truly spiritual. For them, true spirituality has authority and power, not the tentativeness they often feel. However, a Crystal who does not recognize and follow the impetus of his or her life misses an opportunity to develop a deep, meaningful one-on-one relationship with God in this lifetime. If this internal impetus is unheeded, a Crystal's life is one endless stream of emotionally charged but unresolved and unacknowledged situations, leaving a Crystal feeling bereft of God, with no meaning or solace in this life.

Crystals love learning. They are hardworking, conscientious, and diligent. For subjects that hold little interest, such as foreign languages, accounting, and math, a Crystal learns by rote. These subjects seem to require a level of concentration and effort that Crystals find difficult to give. However, in areas of applied creativity, such as interior design, Crystals do remarkably well. In the healing arts—medicine, psychotherapy, nursing, massage, or skin care—they excel. In the arts, Crystals are able to marry their natural talents to the intuitive way they learn.

EMOTIONAL MAKEUP

The aura of a Crystal seems to absorb and refract other colors of the spectrum. The amount of color that collects in this aura is proportional to the other aura colors the Crystal interacts with in a given period of time. For instance, some part of a Crystal's aura will become green when the Crystal interacts with a Green.

Crystals have the ability to camouflage their Personality Spectrums color by absorbing rays of other aura colors. In doing so, Crystals also take on the characteristics and mannerisms, language, thoughts, and behaviors of the other colors.

Family and friends find this confusing, and it can cause break-downs in communication when expectations are not met and responses are not normal. Children of Crystals are confronted with parents who seem inconsistent in their discipline and rules. Parents are puzzled by Crystal children who retreat emotionally, giving no clue as to what they are thinking or feeling. Parents do not know how to relate to a Crystal child from one day to the next.

Emotionally, Crystals do not have a great deal of flexibility. Their emotional responses seem like learned or rehearsed responses rather than spontaneous reactions to situations and people. It is as if they operate, emotionally, from a script. Consequently, Crystals are shy and retiring, preferring to remain in the background where, they hope, nothing will be demanded of them. They know how to play a part, but they are unable to handle a situation spontaneously.

Crystals rely heavily on sources outside themselves, such as family, friends, and neighbors, for approval and support. These contacts provide them with clues as to how they are expected to behave. They often become dependent on others for identity, decision-making, and access to the outside world. Taking on another person's aura color characteristics provides Crystals with a point of reference.

Emotionally, Crystals are very fragile, as if their nervous systems are perpetually on the verge of overload. They tend to be inward-turning as opposed to introspective, for the only safe place they know is that quiet spot deep within themselves. When they do retreat, they leave others trying to guess what happened.

Crystals rarely show their deepest feelings. Even in times of crisis, they do what is proper or right, not necessarily what is thoughtful or spontaneous. They seem to feel that their real feelings will be misunderstood, and they are therefore reluctant to share those deep parts of themselves. This tendency to react to stress by turning inward gives Crystals an aura of coldness, of emotional unavailability.

Because Crystals seem so delicate and fragile, other, more grounded Personality Spectrums colors want to possess them. Yet Crystals belong to no one but God. They feel that they are generally misunderstood and unappreciated by everyone but God. They are not necessarily martyrs, but can sometimes feel overwhelmed by all of the emotional data they seem unable to process.

When devoting their lives to healing causes, this ability to retreat within serves the Crystals well. They are able to heal others by drawing on inner strength uncomplicated by emotional personal involvement; therefore, their work is psychically clean. However, in one-on-one personal relationships, this frigidity causes deep pain and confusion to those who want more than a Crystal can give.

Crystals are basically loners, not because of some deep childhood psychological trauma, but because they prefer it that way. Friends and family must learn to interact with a Crystal in such a way that the relationship is maintained but the ties of responsibility and interdependence are loosened.

SOCIAL STYLE

Socially, Crystals have a difficult time being with others and vice versa. Their shyness and lack of self-confidence and self-assurance cause Crystals to be withdrawn, reserved, and unsure of themselves. They are usually uneasy in a large crowd, and they become easily disoriented and confused in social situations. Because they have so few coping mechanisms, they try to understand what happens to them by placing responsibility on others. They may become hypercritical of themselves and others, undermining their already low sense of self-esteem. Crystal women are self-effacing, usually referring to themselves as "Plain Janes" regardless of their actual physical appearance.

Crystals lack an instinct for proper social behavior. Their sense of protocol is learned from external sources, such as movies, television, books, and other people. As a result, their conversation is filled with words like "should" and "ought." Life for them is like a play. They feel as if they are onstage without a script, unsure of what is expected of them or what the next scene will be all about. The challenge for Crystals is to give up trying to bluff their way through life. They need to quit pretending that they are following the social program that they think they ought to be.

Crystals tend to have a very low sex drive, because to interact sexually means they must co-mingle their aura with another. This deprives the Crystal of their autonomy, individuality, and identity. They retreat emotionally, giving the illusion of frigidity. The paradox for Crystals is that they may enjoy sex, but its aftereffects are so hard on them physically and emotionally that they hesitate to engage in it. If the retreat from sex lasts long enough, the frigidity becomes real. One solution to this problem is for Crystals and their mates to sleep in separate beds. Ideally, Crystals would prefer separate bedrooms. Without a mate who understands this, by early middle age, Crystals are content to dispense with sex in the relationship. They alter their life-style, often choosing to live alone. They choose celibacy because it brings peace, quiet, and the opportunity to tune their lives to their individual biological clocks.

COMPATIBILITY WITH OTHER COLORS

Physical (environmental) Colors

Reds are too physical to understand the Crystals' need for quiet and solitude. Reds think Crystals are trying to put them off, when Crystals only want solace. Reds' need for physical proximity is threatening to a Crystal.

Oranges are the antithesis of Crystals. Where Crystals are delicate, willing to contemplate the miracle of spring, Oranges want to be outdoors, physically confronting all that the Crystals find repulsive—dirt, bugs, and sweat. These two colors have nothing in common.

Magentas love crowds, people, and excitement whereas Crystals want peace and calm. Magentas love parties; Crystals love being alone. Crystals can admire the love of life that motivates a Magenta; they just don't want to participate.

Physical (body) Colors

Yellows are viewed by Crystals as happy, delightful children who are best admired from afar. Crystals are too brittle and too inwardly directed to have much in common with Yellows. The enthusiasm for life that is a hallmark of the Yellows can become tiresome and draining for Crystals when they have to live with it.

Physical Tans and Crystals are both shy, reticent, and unwilling and unable to share their deepest feelings and emotions. Neither of these colors has the skills for intimacy.

Mental Colors

Mental Tans tend to isolate themselves mentally, as Crystals do emotionally. They tend to be one of the less demanding colors when in relationship with a Crystal. The drawback is that because both can be introspective and reclusive, the relationship can become platonic.

Greens are one of the few Personality Spectrums colors that do not seem to fracture or fragment a Crystal's aura. The harmonic vibrations between these two colors is in fact positive and powerful. In relationships with Greens, Crystals are able to gather their energy and move out into the world. Greens understand the Crystals' need for time alone, and they do not interpret this as rejection.

Nurturing Tans love helping other people to realize their potential. Therefore, in a relationship with a Crystal, a Nurturing Tan wants to find out what is wrong and fix it. Just because a Crystal is introspective does not mean that there is anything wrong or that anything needs to be fixed. Sometimes Crystals find that Nurturing Tans cling too much. This makes the Crystals uncomfortable.

Loving Tans have a pattern that is so scattered that Crystals have a difficult time relating to them. While Loving Tans have the best intentions in the world, the disorganization that accompanies every project causes a Crystal anxiety and discomfort. When overwhelmed, Crystals will lose their tempers and make cutting, unkind comments to a Loving Tan, who was only trying to please.

Emotional/Spiritual Colors

Blue and Crystal are the natural antithesis of each other. Blues love to nurture. However, all that nurturing comes with a price—appreciation. Crystals place very little value on all that occupies a Blue, and are not aware of the time, energy, or thought the Blue expends. Therefore, a relationship between these two colors is often punctuated by hurt feelings and stormy silences.

Violets have enough power to easily encompass the Crystal, for which the Crystal is grateful. Violets appreciate the Crystals' sense of inner self, the reluctance with which they share their lives and themselves with others. Because Violets behave similarly, though from a different motivation, these two colors are compatible in many ways.

Lavenders and Crystals are both too intensely solitary to have anything other than a platonic relationship. Even if sexual activity were a part of a relationship between these two colors, it would still be platonic because they would both view sex as a way of meeting a biological need, like eating dinner. Intimacy and warmth would be lacking.

A Crystal mated with a Crystal would be like fingernails on a blackboard. The vibrations between the two would create an intensity that would shatter any relationship.

Indigos and Crystals have a natural affinity for one another. They seem to recognize and appreciate the unique talents and abilities they both have, while not standing in awe of each other. They have the opportunity to create a special relationship.

PERSONAL POWER AND LEADERSHIP STYLE

Because Crystals lack flexibility in social situations, they appear to have little personal power. Their source of power is their ability to retreat inward, keep their own counsel, and give the appearance of aloofness and nonattachment.

In business, Crystals are very good at delivering a consensus report or a project that represents the work of many people, but they are not willing to draw attention to themselves. Therefore, when it is important that a neutral individual be the spokesperson, a Crystal is the ideal choice. The aura of the Crystal will be reflective of everyone who worked on the report.

The Crystals' leadership ability is vested in their ability to heal. Outside the healing professions, they have very little power. Their energy is too easily fractured; they become confused, overwhelmed by their own good intention. They find the world a frightening place. Situations that most people take in their stride cause a Crystal to become agitated and over-whelmed by confusion.

FINANCIAL CHOICES

Crystals are quick to grasp the implications of a situation. Given an overview of economics, for example, they can quickly learn to make sensible, safe decisions. Crystals do not have a flair for making money creatively. Safe, secure, tried-and-true methods such as investing in real estate or managing an existing business serve them best. They do not have the creative, dynamic flair for starting a business, nor are they able to maintain one without help. But given good front-line managers and decision-makers, a Crystal can maintain the detachment necessary for making the difficult long-term deci-sions. New, young companies require more personal involve-ment than a Crystal is prepared to give. A more mature, established company that needs a steward rather than a driven executive is much more appealing to a Crystal. Money and finances are too specific, too real, for a Crystal to deal with comfortably.

With their own money, Crystals are responsible and care-ful. They believe in paying their taxes and all their bills on time. The idea of breaking the law, however insignificantly, causes Crystals to have nightmares. For Crystals, to lose their freedom, to be placed under scrutiny, is abhorrent.

CAREER OPTIONS

Crystals do well in any job that allows them to work alone at a task that they feel adds value to life. They need a structured, quiet environment and a regular routine. They do well, for instance, as reference, medical, technical, or elementary school librarians. They also do well in any office or work situation that requires repetition and attention to detail.

They do well at all jobs in the healing profession, from doctor's receptionist to physician. They have an austere, aloof manner with their patients because they feel they are called to heal, not to entertain. They give quiet dignity to hospices and other alternative forms of patient care.

As spiritual counselors, teachers, or leaders of prayer groups, they are excellent. They lead by example, gently guiding and directing the students along paths to deeper study and understanding. This is not to say that they do well in all forms of teaching. The public school system frazzles their nerves, leaving them confused and disoriented from trying to meet too many people's needs at the same time.

SPIRITUALITY

For a Crystal, spirituality means living a life of serenity that comes from knowing that one day soon they will be reunited in the all-encompassing essence of being.

Crystals are a unique, exquisite, easily shattered Personality Spectrums color with the internal spiritual mechanism for fine-tuning and aligning the healing energies available inside themselves. Crystals and Indigos are unique and separate from the other aura colors. Both have special gifts and talents. With the advent of sophisticated technology, reawakened spiritual quests, and the threatened extinction of the planet, new and different alternatives are needed to solve our world problems. As we move into the twenty-first century, survival of the species will have to depend more on attitudes and beliefs than on technology, intellect, or brute force. This period of our history demands that we alter our emphasis, shift our focus, and develop the sacred side of ourselves, reawakening our spirituality. The Crystal Personality Spectrums color can play a role as one of the bridges to this new paradigm of thought and action. The Crystal's mission in life is to heal—body, mind, and soul.

When Crystals are aligned with their life's work, they are healthy, happy, fully functioning, and at peace with themselves and others. However, when they refuse to acknowledge their gift and work with it, their lives are unhappy, unfulfilled, confusing, and filled with despair. They become lonely and shortsighted, as if they are living only until they can die.

Crystals have experienced and completed all of the other colors' lessons of life. It is as if God said, "I see that Earth is going to need a new breed of healers. Do I have any volunteers?" The Crystal, intuitively recognizing the need, dedicated to healing, agreed to serve. In exchange, the Crystal is allowed to know the joy of a one-on-one relationship with God. To have such a relationship with God requires a psyche of the purest spiritual form, capable of handling high levels of spiritual vibrations. This capacity is the gift and the life work of a Crystal.

Having a limited repertory of emotional behaviors gives Crystals greater latitude in healing situations. They are not bound by the limitations as others see them. They are free to explore other reasons, causes, and entry points into the physical body for healing. Crystals are the connectors, the physical extension cord between God, the source of the energy, and human beings, the utilizers of that energy. A Crystal has the ability to be the transceiver of the signal, narrowing, focusing, and channeling it for use in specific causes and situations. It is as if the Crystal is the funnel into which energy is poured. Then it is transmuted into specific therapies and passed on to clients and patients in many forms.

Absorbing knowledge from many sources, sorting, shifting, cataloging, and organizing their mental inventory of information gives the Crystals long hours of pleasure and satisfaction. It also requires them to live quiet, insular lives away from the confusion of the world. They seem to be in training for a good portion of their lives, only moving into their work during the latter part of life. Physical fragility, emotional vulnerability, and a hostile environment that challenges their work and knowledge have kept many Crystals from being more open about their interests and their gifts.

SIXTEEN

INDIGO

The reality of our world is a shifting, evolving, dynamic energy field. As part of this ecosystem, humanity is growing and developing. As the needs of the whole shift, changes need to be made in the parts that make up that whole. So it is with the auras. A new color—Indigo—has emerged, with skills, talents, and physical characteristics significantly different from those of the other colors. At this time, most Indigos are still children or young adults. I see Indigo children as a new color invested with new talents and abilities that will be necessary for our evolution. These children have unique characteristics for which we can only guess the purpose.

Parents of Indigo children have a special challenge—how to nurture and cultivate their unique children while at the same time helping them exist in the mainstream of contemporary society. The parents of some of these Indigo children will love and support their differences. Other Indigos will not be so lucky. In this chapter, I will be putting forth what I know intuitively about these children.

The significant thing about Indigos is that they have leadership capabilities unlike those we have heretofore experienced. They understand what it means to be a fully actualized human being without having been taught that concept.

The most difficult thing for an Indigo to develop is patience and forbearance. Because they seem to have already grasped what it means to be authentic, they have little tolerance for others who struggle with this issue. Indigos are not without compassion. However, their form of compassion is to give other human beings time and space enough to find their own answers, to come to their own resolutions.

APPROACH TO PHYSICAL REALITY

Indigos have a biochemical system that has differing needs and considerations than other aura colors. Acceptance of their more sensitive systems pays rich dividends for parents.

Indigos seem to register emotional, physical, and psychological input at an unusually high frequency, in the same way some audio equipment is designed to pick up sound waves in the upper ranges. Consequently, their systems reach overload more quickly. This means that they tire more easily, can become confused from too much noise or chaos. Like the Crystals, they have extremely sensitive neural systems. Excessive excitement or prolonged stimulation can cause them to withdraw into themselves. Adults misunderstand this behavior as being contrary or difficult, when it is simply the Indigo child attempting to find emotional respite.

As infants, they are alert from the start. The most frequent comment from parents of Indigos is that the baby was awake, wide-eyed, and curious from the moment of birth. These infants do not seem to have the unfocused eyes of a newborn.

Indigos also seem to require less sleep than other infants. They nap infrequently, and even then sleep fitfully. This often puts a strain on the new mother who expected her baby to sleep for the first three months. Not so for Indigos. Propping them up on a pillow when they are lying on their back seems to allow these infants a more restful sleep. Afternoon naps are usually heavy and deep, as night sleep is for most of us. These children outgrow their need for naps earlier than others do. If they do nap in the afternoon, they frequently stay awake until all hours of the night. They often awaken from night sleep crying or in an irritable mood, especially if roused too abruptly. The result is physical pain, fright, and dislocation; it is as if they have shifted gears too quickly. Gently awakening an Indigo by knocking lightly on the door of the room or by calling the child's name softly over a period of ten to thirty minutes in the morning is a gift of love they will repay with bright, happy dispositions all day.

While they love dairy products like ice cream and cheese, Indigos often have a physical intolerance to cow's milk, which causes upper respiratory congestion, coughs, runny noses, and ear infections. Substituting goat's-milk products will help them be more comfortable.

Because of their unusually sensitive systems, Indigos need an environment that is more placid and quiet than that required by other children. When subjected to extended periods of strenuous stimulation, their nervous systems become easily overloaded, causing them to become irritable and out of sorts. These children are not spoiled. They simply have different needs. One way to assist them is to play classical music of the baroque period, which provides a stimulus for the logical side of the brain so that the intuitive side is free to roam. Meditation music by composers such as Steven Halpern, Kitaro, or Vangelis is also helpful. It allows them to feel more at peace with themselves, able to adapt to the shifts and changes in their environment more easily and quickly.

As infants, Indigos develop at a very rapid rate. In manual dexterity and gross motor coordination they will develop faster than their peer group during the first two years. As they ponder the problems of manipulation, it is as if the observer is seeing the step-by-step thinking process of the Indigo. It is fascinating to watch them as they discover, observe, and interact with the physical world, sorting and sifting data, making decisions, and achieving successes far beyond usual expectations. These children are very gifted, but in a new and different way. They truly want to understand, not for the sake of enhanced self-esteem or for the privileges that come to the gifted child, but because of their natural inquisitiveness.

In temperament, Indigos incorporate both male and female characteristics simultaneously. As a result, post-pubescent Indigos have no attitudes or values about sexuality—heterosexuality, homosexuality, or bisexuality. It is all the same to them. They go easily back and forth between these various forms of sexual expression. They mate soul-to-soul rather than body-to-body. Sexuality is not an expression of masculinity or femininity, but rather the capacity of one human soul to interact with another soul. Sexual expression is a medium of communication so profound that sex for the purpose of physical release only is incomprehensible to an Indigo. They choose their partners carefully, favoring people who intuitively understand the deep spiritual nature of the sexual exchange of energy represented by the sex act. Because an Indigo is renewed spiritually as well as physically by each such experience, they seem to have lower sex drives, finding that fewer but more fulfilling experiences are preferable to many casual experiences.

MENTAL ATTITUDES

Keen intellectual alertness is one of the most gratifying as well as exasperating aspects of Indigos. They are bright and inquisitive, with an intelligence that cannot be measured by traditional psychological tests. Since these children seem to be born knowing everything, they are not asking for information but for verification of the knowledge they already have. It is as if they are testing others to find out if they are trustworthy. They ask thoughtful questions that demand insightful, considered responses. A response such as "Because I said so" or "Things have always been done this way" will only elicit further penetrating questions from an Indigo. Early on, usually before age two, Indigos have a remarkable grasp of abstractions such as time, distance, and space. These concepts are meaningful to them. They are not being precocious; they have a deep need to understand and verify what they know. Because Indigos get to the essence of things, they are not fooled by appearances. When it is time for them to know, they will not be put off. For the adults in the Indigo child's life, there will be no peace until a question has been answered satisfactorily.

The implications for the education of these children are awesome. They are gifted, and unimpressed with their giftedness, so any system that is unresponsive to their needs is in trouble. Independent without being arrogant, they are like solo molecules floating through the space of their reality. They are eager to learn and experience. However, Indigos are inherently unwilling to adapt to a standardized learning pattern. The traditional school system, with its emphasis on lockstep learning, does not work for these children. Indigos' learning process must follow and flow from their own internal rhythm.

Learning for them is not random or haphazard. They learn in a milieu where all information is interrelated and interconnected. Subjects, topics, and ideas cannot exist in isolation for these children. They see the world and ideas as interconnecting pieces of a larger organizational structure. To learn about a given subject without considering the implications in other areas of knowledge is incomprehensible to them. They need to understand how the pieces fit together. Indigo children learn best when they are encouraged to follow their own interests. They have a capacity for pursuing topics deeply rather than skimming lightly over the surface. They resent teacher-imposed decisions as to what and how they should learn. Indigos want to complete one area of study before moving to the next idea, theory, or concept.

To be at the whim of adults who think they know when it is time to clean up is frustrating for Indigos. They need their own special place—their own room, a table, a corner of the family room—where they can keep their projects set up, without having to clean up after each work session.

These children will respond to the gentle reminder that "it will be dinnertime in half an hour—better think about getting ready for dinner." This gives them an opportunity to mentally put a page marker on their thinking process. This is good advice when dealing with all children; it is essential for Indigos.

They think as Loving Tans do—in a matrix pattern, conceptualizing everything simultaneously. Like Loving Tans, who communicate most naturally and easily with these children, Indigos see the whole pattern and all the individual pieces of the pattern at the same time. As a result, they sometimes have difficulty explaining their ideas and images to others. However, they will hammer their listener with data and examples until they have communicated their idea and the listener has expressed comprehension. While Loving Tans share this thinking process, they seem less doggedly determined than the Indigo to get a response from their listener.

The learning needs of Indigos are eclectic and their learning styles are diverse. Learning programs need to be geared to their quicksilver shifts in interest, their need to know principles, and their need to be in charge of their world. When they are bored, frustrated, or intellectually underestimated, Indigos frequently withdraw into themselves and become increasingly unwilling to make the effort to stay involved emotionally or mentally, sometimes even dropping out of school between fourteen and sixteen years of age. They are not arrogant and do not consider themselves brighter or more astute than their peers. They simply want the freedom, with a certain amount of guidance, to pursue their interests and to satisfy their need to know.

Authority figures must respect and contend with the Indigos' individuality. Indigos cannot be coerced into doing anything they do not want to do; they will not simply accept whatever consequences are meted out. Indigos will remain cooperative as long as they are not patronized. They become incredibly stubborn when they feel put down and will cheerfully disrupt an entire classroom.

EMOTIONAL MAKEUP

On many levels, Indigos are never children at all, even though in their early years of development they can be very childlike. They seem more mature than others of the same age, reacting with sympathy and understanding to life's little dramas. Indigo children are more self-contained than other children, needing less interaction with family and peers. They do well if given large amounts of time alone to pursue their own interests and activities. They have active imaginations and often talk to themselves, lost in another reality. They do well in environments that place clear and safe limits on their behavior while not curtailing their need to explore and discover. Before including an Indigo child in the decision-making process, adults need to state clearly the expectations, limitations, and goals. Indigos are quick to cooperate when presented with clear-cut options, limits, and boundaries.

Few of the normal developmental learning steps apply to Indigos, so parents are often at a loss as to what to do to assist, understand, and motivate the Indigo child. These children cannot be emotionally bribed, nor can they be shamed into conforming to social standards and customs. Indigos will accept the consequences of their behavior rather than go against what they believe to be true. Neither can these children be manipulated through guilt. It is not an emotion they seem to understand. Going without meals, being deprived of privileges, giving up toys or activities—such punishments are of no consequence to an Indigo. They are especially meaningless if the adult tries to justify the punishment by saying, "Do this because I say so."

Indigos are very clear about what they want. If an adult give them choices, then the adult must be prepared to follow through. Choices offered and not delivered threaten the credibility of the adults in an Indigo's life. Promises are remembered. Indigos are not fooled by such vague words as "someday" and "soon." They want to know exactly which "someday" or precisely how "soon." Without meaning to nag they will remind you of your promises, which they see as a part of your responsibility to them. They do not hold grudges or resort to emotional blackmail. They simply remember who can be trusted and who cannot.

Indigos are not demonstrative or overly affectionate. They seem to be self-contained. They are cautious with those to whom they give their affection. While relatively content and well behaved, Indigos are not spontaneous or ebullient. It is as if they have seen it all before.

Indigos can communicate openly and spontaneously with only a few people. Early in their lives, they learn to be guarded and selective in sharing their thoughts, ideas, and emotions. They trust only cautiously.

Discarding the old for the new is not easy for Indigo children. For them, newer is not always better. They seem to think that by wearing a garment or playing with a toy, they endow the object with aspects of themselves. To throw it away simply because something new has arrived to take its place, without acknowledging the personal essence instilled in the object, causes deep emotional pain for an Indigo. Parents would do well to initiate rituals around saying good-bye to the old, whether it is an ancient and grubby stuffed animal or the family automobile. These children have an inherent sense of cycles and endings. To ignore this intuitive knowing is to disparage one of the basic gifts of these children.

Indigo teenagers often feel isolated and out of sync with their peer group. Rebellious hairstyles, music, and clothes seem like a travesty to them, a burlesque of an alternate reality. Their sense of loneliness and isolation is similar to that experienced by a minority within a group. In despair, they often retreat into a mist of drugs and alcohol in an attempt to hide from loneliness rather than make a rebellious life-style statement. They know they do not fit the expected pattern, and often they feel like the black sheep or the misfit of family, school, and society. Indigos, at some deep level, understand that we are all interrelated as family, with no dividing lines and no areas of ownership or separation. Seeing so clearly this lack of distinctions, they feel the isolation of their knowing. They are gentle souls looking for a haven and understanding.

SOCIAL STYLE

Indigos will always tell the truth, no matter how brutal it may seem to others. They are not governed by society's rules. They will not behave in a certain way simply because an adult promises them acceptance or love as a reward for doing so. To an Indigo, there is no such thing as guilt. They have no way of understanding guilt because it is not their life purpose to be "good." It is their purpose to find new ways of allowing the rest of us to express ourselves in a way that will allow us to continue to function as a world. Goodness, niceness, and acceptability are values that have no meaning for an Indigo. These concepts are not motivators for them. They will obey a rule because they agree with the moral premise behind it, and they will behave in a certain way because they want to be in a relationship in which sharing and negotiating are required. But they will not obey as a result of coercion. They are able to say no and mean it; no amount of prodding, promising, pleading, or punishing can make them change their minds.

As children Indigos have a social intelligence far beyond their years. As adults, they are very selective about whom they associate with. As they grow older, they find it more and more difficult to explain their differentness, and they choose friends and companions who accept them as they are. Because they are relatively introspective, Indigos do not try out for the cheerleading squad or work toward becoming captain of the football team. They do not have a lot of friends, preferring to be alone rather than to try to conform.

Indigos often choose mates who are their best friends and companions first, and lovers second. They also choose individuals who have strong personalities firmly rooted in contemporary society and reality. Indigos need the buffer of their mate and family to make them feel safe in the world. They need someone they can trust. In an intimate relationship, they do not want to have to monitor their behavior; therefore they choose mates who are sympathetic to their need to communicate soul-to-soul, and to their unwillingness to conform. The gentleness and emotional commitment of the Indigo are the rewards for those who are in a relationship with them.

COMPATIBILITY WITH OTHER COLORS

Physical (environmental) Colors

Reds and Indigos have a healthy respect for each other's honest view of the world. However, the lusty sexuality of Reds is too intense and too pleasure-oriented to communicate deeply and effectively with the Indigo. These colors make better friends than mates.

Oranges think Indigos dropped off another planet. The cool detachment with which Oranges view emotional relationships is an enigma to an Indigo.

Magentas attempt to follow Indigos into their world of imagination and perspective, but seem to miss the first turn.

Whereas Magentas deal with the real world as it is, Indigos deal with the real world as it is becoming.

Physical (body) Colors

Yellows and Indigos love to play together, no matter what their age. The Yellow adds a sparkle of fun, laughter, and joy to the escapades. Indigos appreciate the nonjudgmental acceptance of the Yellows.

Physical Tans are too introspective and too suspicious of what an Indigo represents. Physical Tans like to think they control their environment; Indigos are a direct affront to that notion.

Mental Colors

Mental Tans want to tell Indigos everything in a step-by-step fashion. Indigos just want to know what the fundamental principles are. Indigos tend to regard Mental Tans as prosaic and pedantic; Mental Tans see Indigos as ungrateful and stubborn.

Greens love the multiple connections that Indigos are able to make based on just a small amount of information. Indigos challenge Greens to enrich their fund of knowledge, giving new meaning and a deeper understanding to what they know. Greens challenge Indigos to be more conscientious about details.

Nurturing Tans find Indigos a challenge, one they do not feel equipped to handle. It is difficult enough for them to organize ordinary data without having to deal with the esoteric interests of an Indigo. Nurturing Tans feel inadequate to the task, though Indigos appreciate the quiet acceptance of a Nurturing Tan.

Loving Tans are the natural mentor and teacher for the Indigo at school and in the classroom of life. The thinking processes of these two colors are similar. It is as if the Indigo can see the potential of atomic power as the outcome of the Loving Tan's theory of relativity. These two colors feel a great love and mutual respect for each other.

Emotional/Spiritual Colors

Blues have great tolerance for the inquisitiveness of the Indigo. Indigos thrive in the uncritical presence of the Blues. Each offers the other tolerance and acceptance of their uniqueness.

Violets want to control and dominate the Indigo. The Violet keeps attempting to instill the concept of social guilt in the Indigo, but the Indigo refuses to accept the burden.

Lavenders and Indigos are not willing to be tied down, dominated, or dictated to. Since they both fear being stifled, they respect each other's need for freedom. They both have rich, inner lives.

Crystals love to observe Indigos, and Indigos are responsive to their respect. Crystals and Indigos have compatible interests in spirituality, and they are willing to share their spiritual insights with one another.

An Indigo mated to an Indigo is not an effective match. Both lack the strength to make their way in the world individually or as a pair. They tend to skip over or omit important details.

PERSONAL POWER AND LEADERSHIP STYLE

Indigos are the leaders of the new age because they follow their own inner direction. They will not lead by force, will, or personality. Their power is in their indifference to accepted rewards and their refusal to be manipulated. Indigos will lead by making us rethink and reexamine our beliefs, values, and ways of doing things. By questioning standard practices they will begin to expose the lack of logic in much of what we do. They lack the dictatorial administrative ability of a Violet. They see the alternate realities of the Lavenders and know the changes that are coming in technology, science, and invention. These children are our hope.

The cornerstone of their personalities and of their personal power and leadership style is their refusal to be manipulated or coerced in any way. Once they have decided on a course of action, nothing can dissuade them from pursuing it. No consequence is so severe, no punishment so harsh, as to make Indigos abandon their goals. Indigos are not angry, recalcitrant, or stubborn. They have simply considered all the facts and then made up their mind.

The most important aspect of the Indigos is this adherence to their internal value system, an adherence that seems to be with them from birth. It is not learned or acquired; it just *is*. Indigos are fully actualized human beings who can incorporate all the challenges and potentials of life within themselves. They are born with the knowledge that life is joyful and can remain so, not through avoiding pain, but by accepting it; not by being good, but by confronting lust, greed, and envy and integrating them into one's being.

FINANCIAL CHOICES

Indigos have a very poor understanding of money. They see it as a part of the manipulative system used by some people to control and direct the actions and behaviors of others. Indigos will work because they enjoy the work, because it brings benefit and pleasure to themselves and others, and they feel useful doing it. If they find a job boring, or more work than they bargained for, they will simply quit.

Indigos are not lazy. To observe Indigos working on a project that interests them and absorbs their full attention is to see what tenacity really is. They simply know what they want and what they don't want.

This leaves Indigos in the precarious position of trying to figure out how to support themselves while doing what they enjoy. One of the ways is for them to live communally. Living in a situation where they share expenses and responsibilities works well for them.

CAREER OPTIONS

Currently, Indigos find great satisfaction working with their hands in occupations that require them to pay attention to the process that is not intellectually demanding. Many of them have become artisans, or even repairmen. They are intelligent, soft-spoken, hardworking, and dedicated employees. They take jobs in such industries as construction, plumbing, and electrical contracting, heating, and air-conditioning. They do well in jobs that allow them flexibility and freedom but incorporate limits and guidelines, such as quality control or building inspection.

For the future, as new needs and situations arise, Indigos will move into leadership positions because they have firsthand knowledge gained from experience in repairing today's technology. They will know what we need in the future based on what we have in the present.

SPIRITUALITY

Spirituality as expressed by an Indigo is an example of what it would be like to live without the guilt and fear used by many religions to intimidate and manipulate. Indigos sense the nature of their own divinity, that part of themselves that is a reflection of perfection. Indigos accept their spirituality as a fact of being.

Indigos seem to have been born knowing everything. They seem to come into this existence with all the information of other times, other places, intact. It is as if they remember where they have been prior to coming here. This may be a result of spiritual evolution, or it may be an innate characteristic of the Indigo color.

Indigos have a unique relationship with the Higher Power. Most of us consider the Higher Power to be above us; our spiritual evolution is a process of reaching and striving to elevate ourselves through knowledge, spiritual practices, and examination of our own inner selves. Indigos seem to have an inner sense of the Higher Power. To an Indigo, the Higher Power is a daily reality, not a theological concept. God *is*. Indigos see our striving after spirituality as posturing—much the way Christ saw the Pharisees.

Indigos find it easy to conform to institutionalized spiritual practices. Even as young children they have a gift for spiritual pursuits such as meditation, and an appreciation of ceremonial accoutrements such as incense, medicine rocks, and smudge sticks. They often choose them as playthings. They intuitively incorporate reverence and honor into their behavior, handling the spiritual objects with love and respect. They respond easily and naturally to prayer and meditation rituals; they seem to love the quiet time as well as the space. Indigos are spiritually eclectic, able to incorporate many spiritual traditions, rituals, and symbol systems simultaneously, taking peace and comfort from each. They are not bound by old traditions, habits, or belief systems. These children know that there is an order and a pattern to the universe that has little to do with the rules and regulations others make up. They are able to construct a holistic spirituality within themselves, to build an inner temple capable of accommodating many divergent belief systems.

Because Indigos are born knowing everything, they have easy access to the whole spectrum of what is known in the paranormal or psychic world. Because they know—and know that they know—they are less willing than others to filter out or deny these alternate realities. Many of these children sense the technology of the future. To them, our civilization seems as barbaric and superstitious as King Arthur's court appeared to the Connecticut Yankee.

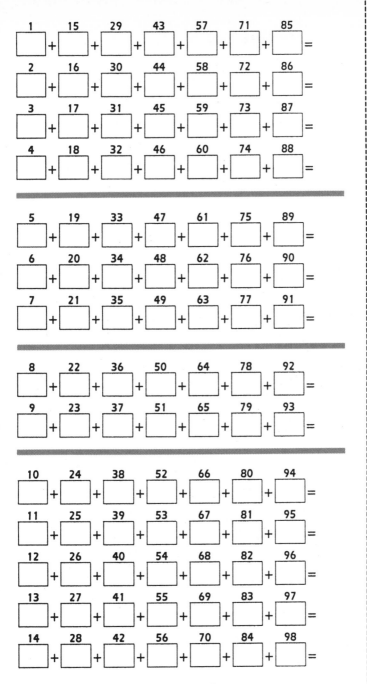

217

TOTAL
[ ]   **MENTAL TAN**

TOTAL
[ ]   **VIOLET**

TOTAL
[ ]   **GREEN**

TOTAL
[ ]   **LAVENDER**

TOTAL
[ ]   **MAGENTA**

TOTAL
[ ]   **BLUE**

TOTAL
[ ]   **NURTURING TAN**

TOTAL
[ ]   **CRYSTAL**

TOTAL
[ ]   **ORANGE**

TOTAL
[ ]   **PHYSICAL TAN**

TOTAL
[ ]   **LOVING TAN**

TOTAL
[ ]   **INDIGO**

TOTAL
[ ]   **RED**

TOTAL
[ ]   **YELLOW**

218

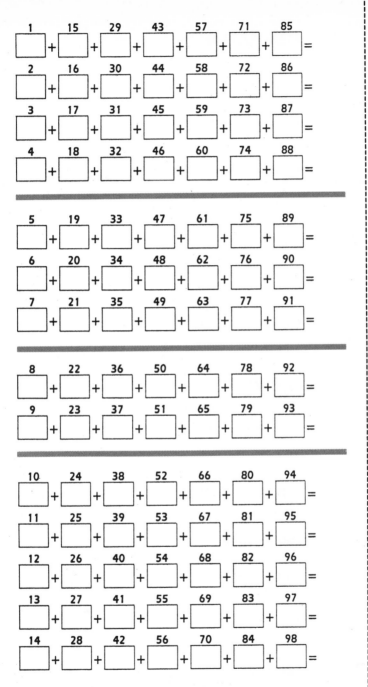

219

FOLD

TOTAL	
	MENTAL TAN

TOTAL	
	VIOLET

TOTAL	
	GREEN

TOTAL	
	LAVENDER

TOTAL	
	MAGENTA

TOTAL	
	BLUE

TOTAL	
	NURTURING TAN

TOTAL	
	CRYSTAL

TOTAL	
	ORANGE

TOTAL	
	PHYSICAL TAN

TOTAL	
	LOVING TAN

TOTAL	
	INDIGO

TOTAL	
	RED

TOTAL	
	YELLOW

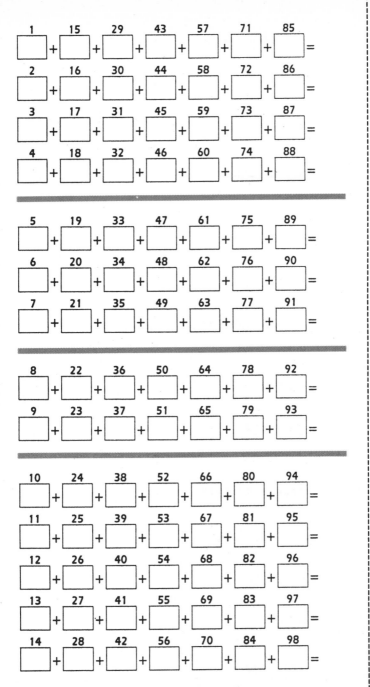

221

TOTAL

[ ] **MENTAL TAN**

TOTAL

[ ] **VIOLET**

TOTAL

[ ] **GREEN**

TOTAL

[ ] **LAVENDER**

TOTAL

[ ] **MAGENTA**

TOTAL

[ ] **BLUE**

TOTAL

[ ] **NURTURING TAN**

TOTAL

[ ] **CRYSTAL**

TOTAL

[ ] **ORANGE**

TOTAL

[ ] **PHYSICAL TAN**

TOTAL

[ ] **LOVING TAN**

TOTAL

[ ] **INDIGO**

TOTAL

[ ] **RED**

TOTAL

[ ] **YELLOW**